A Commentary

Destroying Our Private Cities, Building Our Spiritual Life

Hearing God's Voice from
Paul's Letter to the Philippians

By

Chip M. Anderson

Forward by Phil Callaway, author of
I Used to Have Answers, Now I Have Kids and *Growing Up
on the Edge of the World*

Destroying Our Private Cities, Building Our Spiritual Life
by Chip M. Anderson

Printed in the United States of America

ISBN 1-594672-49-0

Xulon Press
www.XulonPress.com

Xulon Press books are available in bookstores everywhere, and on the Web at www.XulonPress.com.

Some Nice Things People Have Already Said

"I think it appropriate to mention here that I am not customarily a reader of commentaries. I agree with those who have observed that when the angels plan Comedy Night in Heaven, they do not book a humorist, they take turns reading commentaries. This book is a rare exception. You will find in these pages the truths of Scripture handled with care, wrapped in conviction, and rightly divided. This book will not make the angels laugh, but I trust it will cause us all to consider again a book that is as fresh as tomorrow's news."

Phil Callaway, author of *Growing Up on the Edge of the World*

"…a phenomenal book about the fundamentals of the Christian faith as it relates to the Word and the mission of the church. As a minister working with the poor, I frequently encounter Christians who seek to "give" in order to add more meaning and significance to their lives by "helping" someone "less fortunate" than themselves. These "servants" rarely capture what they seek, for in the end they seek something only a dynamic relationship with their creator can provide. Chip clearly establishes this reality with great readable exegetical insight into the letter to the Philippians. His book gives us a great biblical rubric via Paul's letter to the Philippians to understand that seeking our potential has everything to do with serving our savior. This book is a must read, not only for those who are seeking to add true depth to their mission philosophy, but also *their mission activity*."

Reverend Brian Flett, Project Fare-Well Coordinator, Seattle WA

"Chip's lay-commentary on Philippians gives an explanation and meaning to the text with contemporary applications. It is a lively biblical application-driven study of this small four-chapter book. Just reading the section titles whets the reader's appetite to study this book with renewed spiritual interest: Developing a mind for unity and humility; Paying more than lip service to Christian commitment; Christianity found hard but not tried; Adversity is a part of the sanctifying process; Our joy is measured by our love for the church; Joy amid suffering; Christian spirituality is sustained in the arena of community and nourished in the arena of affliction; Servant attributes added; The mind of Christ means pursuing God's glory, not our self-esteem; How do we qualify for honor; Beware a false security; Spiritual formation is molded by humility, not by accomplishment or status; Our level of commitment determines our level of contentment. This book will encourage ordinary Christians to read, understand, and apply God's Word for His glory!"

Doug Nichols, International Director of Action
International Ministries

This work is dedicated to
two ladies in my life
who reveal Christ to me everyday

my mother,
Judy Ann
you're not only a wonderful mother,
but also a beautiful sister in the Lord

&

my daughter,
Amanda Hawley
your initials are carved upon my heart

These ladies remind me everyday that
"God's grace is greater than all my sin."

Table of Contents

Foreword
by Phil Callaway

I was first introduced to Chip Anderson while moderating a debate between Chip and a fellow college faculty member. While the two discussed the issue of whether or not Jesus would appear on religious television (I won't tell you which side Chip took), I, and a thousand others in the audience, couldn't help but admire Chip's style. Rather than chewing up and spitting out his "opponent," Chip sought instead, through gentle humor and admirable wisdom, to win him over.

The very next day I called, asking him to become a regular contributor to *Servant* magazine. Thankfully, he agreed. His column "Real life issues" was a favorite with readers for the same reasons the debate was so popular. Whether listening to Chip or reading his words, one gets the sense that he seems to be wrestling with the issues not just for the reader, but also for himself. Over the years Chip has experienced some of the greatest storms life can blow our way. He has weathered them with grace, courage, and joy, largely because he has made Paul's words to the Philippians a way of life.

The thoughts you are about to read are not some abstract clinical concepts, mastered by a stoic educator. They are truths learned in the school of life by one who has been driven to go deeper, to get past the tired rhetoric and into the living Word of God.

I think it appropriate to mention here that I am not customarily a reader of commentaries. I agree with those who have observed that when the angels plan Comedy Night in Heaven, they do not book a humorist, they take turns reading commentaries. This book is a rare exception. You will find in these pages the truths of Scripture handled with care, wrapped in conviction, and rightly divided. This book will not make the angels laugh, but I trust it will cause us all to consider again a book that is as fresh as tomorrow's news.

Thanks, Chip, for winning me over,

Phil Callaway
Prairie Bible College, Three Hills, Alberta
Editor of *Servant Magazine,* and author of *I Used to Have Answers, Now I Have Kids: What It's Really Like at My House* and *Growing Up on the Edge of the World.*

Author's Preface

G.K. CHESTERTON ONCE REMARKED, "Christianity has died many times and risen again, for it has a God who knows the way out of the grave."

Every time the Church begins to adopt its culture's values, it dies a little. Often it is brought to the brink of the grave. In every age, in every place, the Church has had to wrestle for its very life against the surrounding culture. But the pallbearers have yet to outlive the Church!

The reason is plain. In every generation there are those who read God's eternal Word and respond. They raise the Church above the dying culture around it. The culture ends up occupying the grave, not the Church.

One New Testament letter in particular cuts across the misplaced values of a self-centered culture. That letter is Paul's correspondence to the Philippians.

Historian Will Durant understood the tension existing between the early Church and its surrounding Graeco-Roman culture. He once observed, "Caesar and Christ…met in the arena, and Christ won." The gospel of Christ outlived not only the Roman Caesars, but it has outlived every ruler to date who has raised his or her hand against it.

But therein lies a phenomenon. Jesus Christ never physically confronted Caesar. Jesus Christ has not physically confronted *any* culture. He has left that task to His humble followers who comprise His Church. It was true in the apostolic age. It continues to be true today.

One aspect of our American culture is especially threatening to the Church—that is, our penchant for privatization, for individualism. Simply put, we have shrunk the universe to the size of ourselves. *We,* as individuals, are all-important. *Our* interests, *our* feelings, *our* views are what matter. Nothing else counts.

The Christian community, the Church, historically others-oriented, has succumbed to this cultural virus. The individual North American Christian, rather than Christ, has become the center of Christianity. Our concepts of the Church, sanctification, and spirituality have been relegated to the private sphere.

All of this was happening in the church at Philippi, too, and Paul addresses the issue in his letter. He wanted to lift the Christians at Philippi above the dying culture around them. He wanted to destroy the virus of self-centeredness that was sapping their church life. His letter reminds us that authentic Christian living is not the result of cultural imitation, but the imitation of Christ *and is revealed through our church's communal life.*

The similarities between Philippi in A.D. 62 and present-day North America are what make this letter to the Philippians so especially relevant. My goal in this commentary has been to focus on that relevancy.

I have endeavored to put the drive of Paul's original text in contemporary terms, especially as it confronts our privatized faith. Along with the exposition, I have interacted with some of the prophetic voices of our time who wish to raise the Church above the present-day forces of modernity that mold our view of the world, and rob the Church of its persevering joy.

Please take the endnotes seriously. In them I refer to a number of excellent sources that I have found helpful in my study and application of this Spirit-inspired letter.

Foremost, I want to thank my former students at Prairie Bible College (in Three Hills, Alberta), who persevered in my courses, especially the one I taught on Philippians—for interacting with my interpretations of this Letter long before I put them to print. They helped mold my thinking, but, of course, I take responsibility for my conclusions. Thank you to my friends and family who labored through early drafts of this manuscript, giving insight and suggestions. Thank you for making my thoughts readable!

Phil Callaway, editor of *Servant Magazine,* my very first "real" editor—and still he remains my friend—deserves at least some credit for whatever clear writing abilities the reader may observe. Thanks for taking a chance on my thoughts, my "academic" writing ability, and, of course, me. The columns you allowed me to write for *Servant* were a great experience—hope I didn't get you in too much trouble!

Thanks must also go to the Wednesday evening Adult Bible Study class at Trinity Baptist Church in Fairfield, CT who so willingly plunged into the manuscript as a workbook for a course on Philippians. Nancy, Todd, Mom, David, Bob, Janelle, Boswell, Emily, George, MaryAnne, Denise, Ed, Ray, Ray, Gary, and others who graced us during this hour—I appreciate your patience and the honor to teach you some of my musings on Philippians and how it applies to our Church amid this culture of ours.

Over the years, many people have influenced me to "think the thoughts of God." Chief among them are Ravi Zacharias, founder of Ravi Zacharias International Ministries—his voice and influence will certainly be heard amid my words—and also, Don Alexander, my teacher and mentor at Crown College, St. Bonifacius, MN—his pushing me to struggle with the text can be sensed as well.

I thank God for these people, and countless others. I owe them a great debt. May this present endeavor, in some measure, help all who read it better hear God's Word to us from Paul's Philippian Letter and, thus, to enter more fully into "the mind of Christ." May God empower us to "contend" together "for the faith of the gospel."

Chip Montgomery Anderson
Bridgeport, CT
November 2003

INTRODUCTION

The Philippian Correspondence

IN THE THREE DECADES SINCE the day of Pentecost, the new Christian faith had significantly penetrated the Gentile world. Persecution following Stephen's martyrdom (Acts 6-7) scattered Christians from their Jerusalem enclaves into other parts of Judea and even Samaria (cf. 8:1-8, 25). Perceptibly the Church, at first largely Jewish, took on a distinctly Gentile hue. Roman roads and Roman toleration smoothed the way.

The Road to Philippi
Back in Jerusalem, Jewish authorities had determined to stop the advance of this outrageous heresy at least among Jews. Saul of Tarsus was their enthusiastic point man. They authorized him to bring to Jerusalem as prisoners any Jews in Damascus who were followers of Jesus (9:1-2). God sovereignly intervened, as we know.

That story line changed the course of world history.

Not long after the apostle began taking the gospel to the Gentiles, Saul of Tarsus began to use his Greek name,

Paul. On his second missionary journey, hindered providentially as he itinerated in western Asia, Paul had a vision. A Macedonian stood begging him, "Come over to Macedonia, and help us" (16:9). That vision and Paul's decision to take the gospel into Europe also changed world history.

The first stop for Paul and his missionary team after reaching Macedonia was Philippi. Luke, who by then had joined the group, describes Philippi as "a Roman colony and the leading city of that district of Macedonia."[1]

In Philippi Paul found no Jewish synagogue (his favorite entrée in a new city). But a group of women, possibly Jewish wives of Gentile husbands, met for prayer each Sabbath at a riverfront location. One of the women—Lydia—responded to Paul's preaching (16:13-14). Her decision changed Philippi's history.

That was about A.D. 50. A decade later, Paul was under house arrest in Rome awaiting trial for his faith in Jesus Christ. One of his visitors was Epaphroditus, sent by the Philippian church. Epaphroditus had supplies for Paul, graciously sent by the congregation (Philippians 2:25). Epaphroditus also bore news from the church. Not all of it was good.

The Purpose of the Letter

There were tensions in the church at Philippi. Some of the members were wondering if their faith was able to sustain them (cf. Philippians 4:6, 19). One commentator calls it a combination of "disagreements, distrust, and a poisonous spirit of self-seeking."[2] The church leaders had become fascinated by a false gospel proposed by false Jewish-Christian missionaries (3:2). These teachers brought a Law-based sense of spirituality into the Philippian congregation, thereby eroding the church's confidence. They brought a fair amount of disunity as well. In Paul's eyes, this put the true gospel at risk.

Paul's letter to the Philippians had a dual purpose. First, it was to reestablish Paul's rapport with the Philippian Christians. He wanted to thank them for their support of his missionary and church planting work and for supplying his needs while he was incarcerated. He wished to let them know how he was faring and of his hope for a soon release—so he could return to them!

Second, Paul wrote in order to restore their persevering joy. Although the letter to the Philippians qualifies as a true "missionary prayer letter," the apostle also sought to instruct and exhort the congregation. He hoped his words might return health to their ailing faith. Paul designed every aspect of his letter to help the worshipping community at Philippi walk as worthy citizens of heaven (1:27; 3:20). Paul was determined they should stand steadfast (1:27; 4:1), striving together (1:27; 4:3) for the sake of the gospel.

The Significance of the Letter

Most students of the Bible understand the problems in the Philippian church as theological. That is, the church was attracted to a works-oriented gospel preached by the Judaizers—false Christian missionaries who defined the Christian life through the Mosaic Law. But it is instructive to examine the social and cultural background at Philippi that encouraged such a (false) view of the Christian life.

Jews had found a measure of toleration and protection under Roman law. Even their synagogue and temple worship was designated *religio licita* (a legitimate religion). Jews were excused from participation in civic obligations they found offensive, from the imperial cult functions and from the worshipping of Roman deities. *Not so Christians.*

Moreover, Philippi was named after a Caesar. This Roman colony exalted Caesar like no other city in the empire except Rome itself. All of this set the church and the gospel (almost since day one) at odds with Philippian culture and customs. Christianity was *religio illicita* (an illegitimate religion) because it was antithetical to the imperial cult and the worship of Caesar as lord.

This crisis of culture disposed the congregation toward the Judaizers' false gospel. It would ease their conflict with Rome. It would give them a legitimate social identity and a measure of protection. Most likely, the Judaizers argued, "The Philippians' present status as Christians was incomplete or valueless."[3] Thus the agitators were able to use the Philippians' cultural crisis to lure them to a seemingly more secure basis for their faith. A major purpose of Paul's letter was to restore the Philippians' confidence in the true gospel of Jesus Christ.

The Lordship of Jesus Christ
The lordship of Jesus Christ is a significant aspect of this letter. When Paul preached the gospel in Philippi, he made the Lord Jesus Christ central to what he said (Acts 16:18, 31-32).

The townspeople understood Paul's words as an explicit attack on the emperor. Paul was arrested for proclaiming anti-Caesar ideas (16:19-24).

Thus, right from the start, the gospel put the Philippian church at odds with the surrounding culture. In the church, Roman citizens were attaching themselves to a rival Caesar, a rival Lord.

Paul uses the word *Kurios,* the Greek word for "Lord," fifteen times in this short letter (Philippians 1:2, 14; 2:11, 19, 24, 29; 3:1, 8, 20; 4:1, 2, 4-5, 10, 23). He refers to Jesus as his personal Lord (2:19, 24; 3:8; 4:10). He calls Jesus the Lord of the Church (1:2; 3:1; 4:1, 23). And Paul certainly sounded an anti-Caesar note when he referred to Jesus as the Lord of the universe, the cosmos (2:10-11; 3:2-21).

Sanctification, Lordship of Christ, and the Church

Although Paul does not use the typical terms for sanctification in this letter, the concept forms a definite background for its message. He exhorts the Philippians to "conduct yourselves in a manner worthy of the gospel of Christ" (1:27). The main section of the letter (1:27-4:1) details *how* they are to walk worthy of the gospel. Certainly this involves sanctification.

Although every Christian, by virtue of Christ's death and faith in His completed work, is sanctified before God, we must progress in that sanctification. In the Philippian correspondence, Paul reminds us that our sanctification, our spirituality is intimately connected to the Lordship of Christ. No matter one's particular view of sanctification, all Christians must come to terms with the lordship of Jesus Christ. It is Jesus' lordship that makes the gospel authentic and authoritative. We do not have a divided gospel or a divided Jesus. The adage, "He is Lord of all or He is not Lord at all," has aspects of truth for all believers. Whether concurrent with their salvation or subsequent to it, God will continually confront us with the need to surrender more and more of life to Jesus Christ. Our spiritual growth—sometimes in sweet moments, sometimes in crisis—will always be a confrontation with the Lordship of Jesus Christ.

So, there is the progressive aspect to our sanctification. God more and more separates us *from* the world and separates us *to* Himself. He more and more conforms us to the image of His Son (see Romans 8:29). Most of the exhortations in Philippians deal with this progressive side of sanctification. Thus, true spirituality is a main concern for Paul throughout the letter.

Sanctification and the Christian Community

The work of sanctification does not happen in a vacuum. There are two opposing elements operative in believers' spiritual progress. On the one hand, believers are at odds with the world—the surrounding sin-marked culture. They are tempted to relieve this tension by adapting their faith to the surrounding culture. Thus they hope to feel more comfortable, more at home. God's work of sanctification, however, is conforming them to His Son (Philippians 2:5-11; 3:8, 10). This means a continued measure of discomfort as long as they exist "in the world" (1:27ff).

On the other hand, sanctification is a community project. As we read Philippians, we cannot escape the centrality of the Church. The work of sanctification takes place in that setting, *within the community of believers.* As believers grow spiritually, the Church becomes more and more significant for them.

Joy and the Christian Frame of Mind
Finally, in Philippians there are the obvious references to *joy.* These references permeate the letter (1:4, 18, 25-26; 2:2, 17-18, 28-29; 3:1; 4:1, 4:4, 10). They must have captivated the Philippian Christians, even as they captivate us. Christians are called to a life on the joy side. It is this joy in Christ that Paul wishes to restore to the Christian community in Philippi. External tension with the culture and internal tension among the believers had conspired to diminish their supply of joy. That, in turn, limited their will to persevere.

To restore the joy personally and in their Christian community, Paul repeatedly exhorts the Philippians to have a correct, Christian "frame of mind" (1:7, 27; 2:2, 5; 3:15, 19; 4:2, 10). Their mind-set was to match Christ's. He "made himself nothing, taking the very nature of a servant" (2:7). He "humbled himself and became obedient to death even death on a cross!" (2:8). Such an attitude marks the gospel of Christ and should mark our spiritual journey. Such an attitude provides the incentive and the content for restoring the Church's health and the Christian's persevering joy.

We know little concerning the impact of this letter on its first readers, the beleaguered, somewhat discouraged Christians in Philippi. But in the more than nineteen centuries since Paul's Spirit-inspired words were set to parchment, they have brought significant changes to individuals and communities of believers. These words can change your life and your church's life—and even perhaps, the life of the community where you live, work, and play.

> *May the mind of Christ, my Savior,*
> *Live in me from day to day,*
> *By His love and power controlling*
> *All I do and say.*
> *May I run the race before me,*
> *Strong and brave to face the foe,*
> *Looking only unto Jesus*
> *As I onward go.*
> *May His beauty rest upon me*
> *As I seek the lost to win,*
> *And may they forget the channel,*
> *Seeing only Him.*

(Kate B. Wilkinson, 1859-1928)

Endnotes

[1] See the introductions in Gerald F. Hawthorne, *Word Biblical Commentary,* Vol. 43, *Philippians* (Waco, TX: Word, 1983); Gordon Fee, *Paul's Letter to the Philippians* (Grand Rapids, MI: Eerdmans, 1995) and Moises Silva, *Philippians* (Chicago: Moody, 1988).

[2] Silva, 4.

[3] Mikael Tellbe, "The Sociological Factors Behind Philippians 3:1-11 and the Conflict at Philippi," *The Journal for the Study of the New Testament* 55 (1994): 97-121.

CHAPTER 1

Destroying Our Private Cities
Philippians 1:1-2

Paul and Timothy, servants of Christ Jesus, to all the saints in Christ Jesus at Philippi, together with the overseers and deacons: Grace and peace to you from God our Father and the Lord Jesus Christ.

MY GIRL FRIEND FROM COLLEGE WAS STAY-ING with her sister and brother-in-law for the weekend. She was on an assignment for her course in child psychology. Her project: Observe how little children interpret the world around them.

One of the observations was unplanned. Her four-year-old nephew, Ben, unashamedly opened the bathroom door and entered, to the surprise of his aunt. Although a bit startled, his aunt was able to use the occasion to help Ben understand the concept of privacy.

"Ben, when people close the door, that means they

would like to have their privacy." Ben acknowledged his aunt's instruction and went his way. The issue seemed to be settled.

Later that afternoon, Ben's mother noticed his bedroom door closed. That was a bit unusual, she thought. She proceeded to open it to check on her son.

"Ben, are you all right?" she asked in a tone of concern.

Ben looked up and in a matter-of-fact voice said, "Mom, I closed my door because I want my own *private city.*"

That serendipity is as instructive as it is winsome. It is both appropriate and polite to respect another's privacy. But there comes a time in a culture when the concept of privacy can hinder the equally appropriate sense of community. It can stifle cooperative participation in the responsibilities of the community. Attitudes such as *my world, my choice* eventually produce the pursuit of *personal fulfillment.* Like young Ben, people today seem to crave their own private city.

Our Privacy Bent Has Bent the Church

This plague of privacy has had a devastating impact on the Church and its mission. North American Christians have embraced our culture's fascination for privacy, at the same time ignoring its consequences. Because we treasure our "private cities," we are governed not by the will of God or the Scriptures but by personal fulfillment. And we view life from a very narrow perspective. Our Christianity becomes trivial and private because we relegate it to the private sphere of our lives.

Guinness, in his book *The Gravedigger File,* laments that Christianity to the believer

...was once life's central mystery, its worship

life's most awesome experience, its faith life's broadest canopy of meaning as well as its deepest guarantee of belonging. Yet today, where religion still survives in the modern world, no matter how passionate or "committed" the individual believer may be, it amounts to little more than a private preference, a spare-time hobby, a leisure pursuit.[1]

This worship of privacy has had devastating consequences for the Church's participation in the missionary task. I have worked with many mission leaders. Almost every one of them have voiced a grave concern about the future of missions as they look upon contemporary missionary candidates. They know there is an all-time-high attrition rate among first-term missionaries. The reason given most, "Young people go into missions in order to find personal fulfillment."

Christians have been so captivated by our culture's love affair with privacy that the gospel and world missions have paid a heavy price. When our own "personal fulfillment" is the center of Church life, the gospel of fulfillment replaces the gospel of Jesus Christ. Paul's letter to the Philippian church puts a torch to the Christian's "right to privacy" and ignites the Spirit's passion among us to be participants in the work of the gospel.

Spiritual Growth Implies the Overthrow
of Privatized Faith

Many have observed the numerous times Paul uses the words *joy* and *rejoice* throughout the letter (1:4, 18, 25-26; 2:2, 17-18, 28-29; 3:1; 4:1, 4, 10). This has led some to conclude that Paul's theme in this letter is joy in Christian living. But we should not let such a conclusion obscure a more central concern throughout the letter.

Paul's theme revolves around the relationship of the gospel to the Church. Rivalry and conflict over status and spirituality had crept into the congregation. The apostle seeks to rectify their misplaced thinking with right thinking—the Christian mind. This effort on Paul's part is underscored by his repeated use of the verb *to think*—*phroneo*—throughout the letter (1:7; 2:2, 5; 3:15, 19; 4:2, 10). English versions translate *phroneo* in a variety of ways: "feeling," "attitude," "harmony," "concern." These mask Paul's emphasis in calling the Philippian church to proper Christian thinking about themselves and the work of the gospel. We are to have a proper *frame of mind* for the sake of the gospel.

Paul's frequent use of *joy* is a rhetorical device to stimulate a mutual sense of comradeship (the real issue). Joy is the enemy of disunity and strife. Christ-like thinking is the key to unleashing the church for its mission. In order to grow spiritually and overthrow our "private cities," we must develop a mind for unity, a mind for humility and a mind for the gospel.

Developing a Mind for Unity
Someone commented that if only the salutation of this letter had made it to Philippi, there still would be abundant apostolic instruction. Those two introductory verses indicate Paul's tone and his purpose for writing:

> *Paul and Timothy, servants of Christ Jesus,*
> *to all the saints in Christ Jesus at Philippi,*
> *together with the overseers and deacons:*
> *Grace and peace to you from God our Father*
> *and the Lord Jesus Christ.* (1:1-2)

Paul deliberately opens his letter to the Philippian church with greetings to "all the saints" and to the church's "overseers and deacons" (1:1). Nowhere else in the apostle's letters does he address such a specific group as the overseers and deacons. The combined emphasis and juxtaposition of "all" the saints and the singling out of the leadership is significant. It suggests that some form of disunity or rivalry within the congregation was threatening the gospel. It may have been the leaders who were causing division. Or perhaps it was coming from some outside source. Or—still more likely—it may have been a combination of the two. But Paul knows that unity within a congregation is essential to the successful fulfillment of that church's mission.

The Philippian congregation was born through Paul's missionary efforts (Acts 16). Ever after, the members had taken a strong interest in his continued missionary work, providing financial and material support (Philippians 1:7; 2:25-30; 4:15-16). Paul was delighted to boast of this support to other churches (2 Corinthians 8:1-5; 11:7-9). But now, some people had covertly infiltrated the ranks. They had fractured the unity and single-mindedness that had fostered such a strong commitment to the spread of the gospel.

Throughout the letter Paul calls the congregation back to *right thinking.* He calls them back to right thinking about themselves, about their leaders, about their opponents and about the gospel itself. He shows the Philippian congregation that right thinking will banish disunity and rivalry. It will provoke a single-mindedness for the mission of the gospel (Philippians 1:27; 2:1-5). Paul is affirming his Lord's own words to the disciples that unity is a prerequisite for witness:

> *They are not of the world, even as I am not of it. Sanctify them by the truth; your word is truth. As you sent me into the world, I have sent them into the world. For them I sanctify myself, that they too may be truly sanctified.*

My prayer is not for them alone. I pray also for those who will believe in me through their message, that all of them may be one, Father, just as you are in me and I am in you. May they also be in us so that the world may believe that you have sent me. (John 17:16-21)

Paul's first and primary concern is for the gospel of Jesus Christ. All else is secondary. He knows that a disunited church cannot have the character and strength to be on the cutting edge of gospel proclamation. Disunity shifts the emphasis to selfish concerns such as pride and place and status. Pursuing personal fulfillment and entitlement diverts members from God's primary concern: the spread of the gospel. They must forget the past with all its pride and status, based on worldly standards. They must press forward toward the upward call of God in Christ (Philippians 3:12ff). Only in this way can they unleash their potential as a church to work with one mind for the sake of the gospel (1:27).

Developing a Mind for Humility
How does a person find this mind of Christ? How does a church purge the selfish spirit of the times so that the Spirit of God has freedom? Paul, writing under the Spirit's inspiration, does not answer those questions flippantly. He suggests no easy, step-by-step solutions. He hints at the answer in his opening salutation when he calls Timothy and himself "servants" of Christ Jesus. Two keys are needed to unlock the Spirit's passion for the gospel. One is a shared partnership in the work of the gospel. The other is "humility" of mind (2:3).

Do not overlook Paul's inclusion of Timothy, his travel companion and disciple, as co-writer. Timothy may not actually have co-authored the letter. But the appearance of his name is both strategic and illustrative of Paul's solution to the rivalry at Philippi. Timothy was a partner with Paul in the gospel. This young disciple was an active participant in the spread of the gospel through Macedonia (Acts 16-18), including Philippi. And he provided support for Paul in his imprisonment (Philippians 2:20-22). Paul's mention of Timothy as co-sender of the letter reinforces the idea of teamwork. Paul, father of the Philippian church, was a team player. He was a fellow minister of the gospel with others (1:5, 7; 2:19-30; 4:10, 15-16). Members of a team are interdependent. On a true team, there is no room for rivalry.

Most English translations of 1:1 begin the letter as does the NIV: "Paul and Timothy, servants of Christ Jesus." Actually, the *doulos* word group denoted more than "servants," as we have come to regard the term. In the Roman Empire it stood for a group of people who were literally owned by others. They had subservient roles in society.[2] "Slave" would be a more appropriate translation. We must keep this in mind throughout the letter.

A Striking Omission

A striking omission in the letter's salutation is Paul's usual designation of himself as an apostle. Instead, Paul emphasizes his and Timothy's position as "slaves" of Jesus Christ. In two other letters, Romans and Titus, Paul uses the designation "slave," but there he also identifies himself as an apostle. The significance here takes on a special quality that reinforces Paul's concern for the church and the spread of the gospel. He replaces his rightful apostolic title with the lowly, self-designation of a slave. He does so because humility is of foremost importance in having the mind of Christ (Philippians 2:3, 8). Paul is implying that Timothy and he—and every Christian—belong to Another: to Jesus Christ the Lord (1:2; 4:23).

God has given me the privilege of teaching and serving some of those who will be church leaders in the future. In the Bible college where I taught, I spent many hours outside the classroom discipling students. For whatever reason, I attracted some of the so-called mavericks. I appreciated their novel, nontraditional ideas and their determination to "get the job done." But I also knew that some of their independent spirit could cause more hurt than help. I frequently reminded them that maverick horses have a habit of kicking down barns and harming their would-be riders.

There is a tendency today to value the maverick spirit. We celebrate the Lone Ranger types who have all the energy and single-heartedness to accomplish their visions. But such independence should never be exercised at the expense of others, especially other members of the team.

When Paul writes to the "overseers and deacons" (1:1), he most likely is not referring to two offices of the church. A.D. 62 seems rather early in church development for such distinctive offices to be recognized. More precisely, Paul has in mind "overseers who serve." Thus Paul continues to emphasize his concern for the unity of the church body and its participation in the gospel. The gospel and the church's mission are the great equalizers.

The apostle Paul is grateful for the Philippian church's participation in the work of the gospel (1:3-7; 4:14-18). This gratitude is no mere reference to Paul's disposition toward his Philippian "children" in the Lord. We must remember that Paul's primary concern is for the gospel. His understanding of the Church is wrapped up in its defining character as the sole and dynamic expression of God's fullness on earth (Ephesians 1:22-23; 4:11-16). When Paul addresses the church as "saints" (Philippians 1:1), he is referring to them as God's people, uniquely consecrated to Him and bound by covenant to be His ambassadors to the rest of the world (Exodus 6:7; Deuteronomy 7:6; 2

Corinthians 5:20). The Church is comprised of the people of God in a place where His kingdom is to be communicated clearly and with power. It is not coincidental that Paul wrote the Philippian church to have joy in their Christian service.

The condition of the Church is of vital interest to Paul. It is to bear witness to the truth of the gospel. The Philippian church was located in a very strategic area, geographically and politically. Philippi, a Roman colony along the Egnatian Way, was not far from the port of Neapolis. It participated in the daily traffic of commerce, culture and religion that flowed from east to west across the Roman Empire. The Philippian church held a key place in the mission of God. Thus its unity and integrity were indispensable.

Robert Bellah and some of his fellow sociologists, in their book, *Habits of the Heart,* explain how modern social values have affected us. The team asked people how they related to this world. When questioned about their work and its meaning in their lives, many responded in terms of personal fulfillment and advancement. When asked about their marriages, they defined them in terms of personal development. When the inquiry turned to church life, many again responded in terms of personal fulfillment.[3]

A Privatized Faith Is Noxious to Spirit-given Unity
The gospel is not the gospel when it becomes privatized. It is not the gospel when it is sacrificed to the spirit of the times. A privatized faith is inimical to Spirit-given unity in the Church. And without that unity, no church will know the mind of Christ.

It is this mind of Christ that the apostle seeks to reinstall at Philippi. He works on the whole Philippian church (Philippians 2:1-11). He works specifically on the leaders (4:2-3). He wants them to know that cultures can and do change; only the gospel endures. Someone remarked that the man who marries the spirit of the age soon finds himself a widower.[4] Whenever the gospel becomes subservient to the spirit of the times, the Church digs its own grave.

Paul surrounded himself with those who were dedicated to the mission of the Church and loyal to his leadership. He knew that others had a different mind. He comments that "everyone looks out for his own interests, not those of Jesus Christ" (2:21). This description underscores how *we* are to think about *our*selves and the mission of the Church today. Christians who surrender their commitment to the gospel and give themselves to the spirit of the times commit two offenses. They sacrifice their own spirituality, and they put those who are outside the Church at deadly eternal risk.

Paying More Than Lip Service to Christian Commitment

The Church has always struggled with the unending shift of culture. The Church must avoid one particular danger. It must not become so like the culture that it cannot confront society's ungodly actions and attitudes. Philippians is God's eternal word to the Church. This word counters perilous spiritual pride and rivalry of status dictated by the spirit of any age. It restores the repentant Church to the place of God's blessing and power.

In this letter Paul demonstrates his strong and willing commitment to the gospel (1:3-20). He evidences also a total allegiance to the welfare and task of the church (1:22-26). Too, he calls Christians to imitate his commitment, his life. They are to show their faithfulness to the Lord of the Church by serving the gospel through the Church. They are to walk as worthy citizens of God's kingdom (1:27; 3:20). They are to stand firm (1:27; 4:1), striving together in the cause of the gospel (1:27; 4:3).

The nature and definition of the Church cannot be separated from its primary task and participation in the spread of the gospel. In Philippians, the apostle Paul confronts the attitudes of pride and self-serving individualism that can destroy the impact the gospel can have on a local community, not to mention hinder its outward movement to the ends of the earth. He seeks to help the Church think right about its first call, its priority commitment to the gospel of Jesus Christ.

Endnotes

[1] Os Guinness, *The Gravedigger File* (Downers Grove, IL: InterVarsity Press, 1983), 72.

[2] Gordon Fee, *Paul's Letter to the Philippians* (Grand Rapids: Eerdmans, 1995), 62-63.

[3] Robert N. Bellah, et. al., *Habits of the Heart: Individualism and Commitment in American Life* (New York: Harper and Row, 1985).

[4] Herbert Schlossberg, *Idols for Destruction: Christian Faith and Its Confrontation with American Society* (Nashville, TN: Thomas Nelson, 1983), 9.

CHAPTER 2

Character Does Matter
Philippians 1:3-11

*W*ALL STREET GREED AND CORRUPTION
DISCLOSED. The headline splashes across page one
of newspapers from Boston to Los Angeles. *POLITICIANS
DEBATE THE CHARACTER ISSUE.* These and similar
stories break regularly on newscasts and in our magazines.

Should we be surprised that a society bent on sepa-
rating every vestige of religion from its public life is
concerned about morals? No. Character *does* matter.

We Christians, of course, know it matters. Our
strength of character and our moral disposition affect our
work, our family, our witness—and the progress of the
gospel. It is an inescapable fact: Character is of primary
concern for the Church and our task of proclaiming the
gospel. But how do we build strong, positive, Christlike
character?

For a time I served as a professor at Prairie Bible
College in Three Hills, Alberta. The president, there, was
rightly anxious that college staff be concerned about student
character development. At one staff meeting he projected an

overhead picturing three bowls. The bowls were labeled *knowledge, skills,* and *character.*

"If we had, figuratively, 100 beans to give the students in their educational and campus-life experiences," he asked, "how should they be distributed?"

"Fifty in character, twenty-five in skills, and twenty-five in knowledge," one person timidly spoke out.

"Five in knowledge, seventy-five in character, and twenty in skills," insisted another.

"Place all 100 beans in the character bowl," suggested a third.

And I, a lowly associate professor sitting in the back of the room, wanted desperately to shout, "Your three bowls bias the results!"

Certainly skills must be developed actively. Yet skills and character cannot be separated from knowledge. The issue is not so many beans in the skills and character bowls versus so many in the knowledge bowl. Rather, we should be asking, "What knowledge do we teach in order to develop godly, Christlike character?" Character is built on the knowledge we are committed to. What we believe— really believe—determines our strength of character. And our character will influence how we use our skills, whether foolishly or wisely, whether for good or evil, whether for personal gain or to extend God's kingdom.

Who we are and what we do with our lives *is* a knowledge issue. The knowledge we are committed to will affect our lives for good or bad. And it will affect the welfare of others.

In Philippians 1:3-11, Paul's prayer reveals his heart for the church. The apostle already knew the church in Philippi was in need of unity, humility, and mutual concern. He desired to lift that group of believers above the pressures of life that produce turmoil for the soul and create havoc with the church's task of ministering the gospel. To all of us who read these Scriptures God is urging us to strengthen our character, not just for morality's sake, but for the sake of the gospel. Through Paul's prayer we discover keys for developing Christ-centered, Spirit-empowered character.

Character Is Built on Our Common Commitment to the Gospel

"All for one and one for all." In the classic *The Three Musketeers,* author Alexandre Dumas portrays an attractive blend of individualism, team spirit, and commitment to a common cause—the king's honor. Each musketeer values the individual's uniqueness but places the whole group's purpose and existence above all else—even life itself. This unity and common commitment play well in fiction, but it is not how life normally works, at least in our Western culture.

Although there is some merit in rugged individualism, the stance generally contributes more to personal fulfillment than to group benefit. Today we nourish the cult of the ego and prize above all else the significance of the individual. This is true in the workplace, in our educational halls, in politics, even in church life. We praise—and otherwise reward—the individual who produces the most or who has the most to give. When the church gets caught up in this kind of "character building," the result is a commitment to individual prowess, not to the Church's ultimate goal and task of ministering the gospel.

What can motivate us to live above these voices that feed our egos, that threaten our families, that militate against God's gospel? What commitment will lift us above the sorrows and afflictions of this life that come to all of us?

Amid the apostle Paul's own hardship he reflects on the Philippians' participation in the work of the gospel (1:5). The word Paul uses to describe this partnership is *koinonia.* This word carries connotations of companionship, sharing, holding in common, participation, fellowship. The church is to be devoted to fellowship (Acts 2:42) because of our common relationship in God's Son (1 Corinthians 1:9). This close bond and common commitment among believers is supernaturally experienced through the work of the Holy Spirit (2 Corinthians 13:14). When believers do not value their Christian fellowship and mutual partnership in the gospel, their character forfeits its strength.

Paul's Self-value Is Locked Up in the Gospel

It is this common commitment to the gospel, this partnership with others, that lifts Paul above his unjust incarceration to rejoice that nothing—even confinement—can stop God's work (Philippians 1:12-18). Paul's self-value is locked up in the gospel, not the injustice of persecution. Paul derives strength of character not from the decree and power of Caesar but from the decree of the true King, Jesus Christ, in whom the good news is centered.

Paul sets his mind on the fact that the gospel—the cause he is committed to—continues despite personal setbacks and hardship. No one individual is indispensable. We exercise our cultural bias when we prize our fulfillment and self-satisfaction above the well-being of others. This tends to lead to rivalry of status. When we don't receive "our due recognition," our hearts become filled with turmoil and strife. Full commitment to the cause of Christ gives our lives proper perspective. It also encourages others in the knowledge that they are not alone.

There is another interesting thing about this *koinonia,* this fellowship in the gospel that Paul has been alluding to. It is not limited to those specially designated tasks that we think of as full-time vocational ministries. The partnership Paul is referring to here is broad. Not only did the Philippians help finance Paul's church-planting efforts, but they also supplied his needs for clothing and food while he was under house arrest. Our participation in the gospel is as extensive as our creativity allows it to be. Christian ministry can be as far-reaching as our imaginations permit.

The gospel is simple. It is the task of our King—the spread and increase of the announcement of redemption through Christ Jesus. Our partnership in this task can be expressed in a multitude of creative ways. When there are no indispensable people and no special interests, our lives will draw meaning from our relationship to Christ. Our character will be strengthened by our working for a common cause—the honor of the King!

Character Gains Confidence by Trusting God's Abilities

The Philippian believers began their participation in the task of the gospel at the very time Paul planted the church there (1:5). However, like the Galatians, the Philippians were in danger of trying to complete by the flesh what they began in the Spirit (Galatians 3:3). The Galatians' fleshly pursuit of perfection led to a compromised gospel. The Philippians' flirtation with the flesh led to a pursuit of status and rivalry.

In Philippians 1:6, it is difficult to decide whether Paul is talking about the Philippians as individual Christians or about the Philippian church as a whole. The text could be rendered, "I am confident...that he who began a good work in [each one of] you will carry it on to completion until the day of Christ Jesus." Or it can be understood in a corporate sense: "I am confident...that he who began a good work in you [the Philippian church] will carry it on to completion until the day of Christ Jesus." It is popular today to personalize Scripture. But elsewhere in the letter Paul focuses on unity, humility, and mutual concern among the corporate Philippian believers. It seems more likely, therefore, that he is addressing here the Church as a whole. He is directing their attention to God's ability to complete the work of the gospel through the Church.

Our confidence will be on shaky ground if it is built on human resources. Although Paul is encouraged by the Philippians' partnership in the gospel, his confidence is grounded in God's powerful, unchanging character. Paul's ability to ascend above life's cheap shots is not dependent on human abilities or resources, but on the character and achievements of God.

Looking Beyond Rome to Christ's Return

While under house arrest in Rome, Paul casts his mind's eye beyond the horizon. He looks far beyond imperial Rome, beyond the corrupt Roman society, beyond false teachers invading the church, beyond the church's flirtation with pride. He looks to the return of Christ. Paul is confident that God's work through the church will continue uninterrupted until that final day.

Long after the church in Philippi is ancient history, God will continue to bring about the power of salvation through His ever-expanding Church in the world. He knows that "the God of peace" will continually sanctify the Church in every age, helping it to persevere until the coming of our Lord Jesus Christ (1 Thessalonians 5:23). This confident expectation brings comfort, assurance, and fortitude in the midst of trial.

We live in a narcissistic environment. When the pressures of life begin to overtake people, they tend to turn inward. Christians are inclined to the same temptation. Like our non-Christian counterparts, we too tend amid hardship and affliction to reach for human resources. Because we seek to protect ourselves from further harm, we begin to trust in what we can see and feel rather than in the God who promises to keep His word. Christlike character is developed not by the absence of suffering but by persevering through it. Thus we must build strong Christian character by trusting in the immovable, unshakable, never-changing, consistent God of the Bible. He will accomplish His work of building His Church "until the day of Christ." If you are incorporated into the Church, the Body of Christ, you can have confidence that God will not abandon the work He has begun (Philippians 1:6). Paul knew, despite his incarceration, that he was a part of God's Church. Therefore he had confidence to persevere. It is such confidence that develops strength of character that lifts us above the travail of living "in the world."

Character Is Enriched by a Common Sense Love
Paul's confidence in God's ability to build the Church unshakable and unconquerable motivates him to pray that the Philippians' "love may abound" (1:9). He knows that if the love they already possess continues to grow, it will overtake and subdue existing pride and rivalry. Their Christlike character will overflow in kindness, caring and humility— attitudes that will resolve the problems that hinder the work of the gospel.

Our character will be measured by our love for others, a commitment that produces concern for people other than ourselves (cf. 2:1-4). Paul told the Galatian believers that the Holy Spirit produces an inner love that humbles rather than exalts selfish pride (Galatians 5:19-23). He declared to the Corinthians that loveless Christianity is tantamount to a "resounding gong or a clanging cymbal" (1 Corinthians 13:1). Prideful convictions and loveless orthodoxy produce friction in the household of God and disinterest among the unchurched.

The ambiguity of the word *love* makes talking about it difficult. John Stott rightly says,

> Nothing perhaps is more harmful than the
> easy good nature which is willing to tolerate

everything; and this is often mistaken for the Christian frame of mind. Love must fasten itself on the things which are worthy of loving, and it cannot do so unless it is wisely directed.[1]

Paul Prays that the Philippians' Love Will Abound

Paul gives weight to the Christian concept of love by telling the Philippians what he is praying for. "This is my prayer," he says, "that your love may abound more and more in knowledge and depth of insight" (1:9).[2] Love that feeds on the desires of selfishness will produce a weak and malnourished character that cannot withstand the pressures of life. True Christian love will be tempered by biblical knowledge and godly common sense.

Our love must be rooted in the fear and reverence of God (Proverbs 1:7). If our gospel is to have relevance and our witness integrity, our Christian love will produce actions that benefit others.

Paul is not praying for mere head knowledge but knowledge that flows from a reverence for God. It is knowledge manifested by a biblically informed, godly common sense. Our love is not all-embracing and touchy-feely. It is a love that flows from our Christlike character, permeating the fabric of our church and community life. A wise love "trained...to distinguish good from evil" (Hebrews 5:14) gives us the ability to make proper moral decisions in the face of conflicting choices.

Philippians 1:10 points out the result of such love tempered by genuine, godly knowledge and common sense: "so that you may be able to discern what is best and may be pure and blameless until the day of Christ."

In order to be the best people possible and to make the best choices in life, Christians must grow in the knowledge of God and the wisdom of heaven. In our church and public life we will be called upon to make a multitude of choices. We are to be motivated by the broad plan of God to influence and win the world for Christ (1:5-7). So our choices in this life must stem from our commitment to the Church's task of *proclaiming* the gospel. We must place our selfish ambitions underneath our concern for others. Godly love for others enables us to discern not only the good from the bad, the moral from the immoral, but also the important from the unimportant.

Character Must Be Grounded in Christ
Albert Klasky was one of my best friends while I was serving in the U.S. Air Force. During that time, our friendship revolved around a mutual concern to grow in our Christian faith. I had read A.B. Simpson's *Fourfold Gospel,* and I thought Al would appreciate it. A few days later, he came to my room and sat down on my roommate's bed, grinning ear to ear. (That's more than an over-used figure of speech. Al can really do that!)

>Finally he spoke. "I'll go!"
>"You'll go where?" I asked.
>*"Anywhere,"* he answered. "I just finished the chapter on 'Our Coming King.' I decided to commit myself to missionary service!"

Al and his wife, Theresa, eventually found themselves living among the Fulani people in Mali, West Africa. The picture of Christ's return and the plight of people in need of Christ produced in Al a life committed to the task of the Church. It took my friend fifteen years to get to West Africa, but God used that time to develop and strengthen his character.

Living in the age of McDonald's and ATMs gives us the impression that our spirituality and Christian character should be instantaneous. Paul prayed that the Philippians' love might "abound more and more," implying that their character was to be sanctified progressively.

In 1:11 Paul indicates that this sanctification should be productive: "filled with the fruit of righteousness that comes through Jesus Christ—to the glory and praise of God." It is possible to test our love, the progress of our sanctification, to see whether or not it stems from God and His Word.

Elsewhere Paul reminds us that the Spirit-filled life will produce "love, joy, peace, patience, kindness, goodness, faithfulness, gentleness and self-control" (Galatians 5:22-23). These qualities are not mere feelings or temperaments. They are verbal nouns. The "fruit" is the "truly good qualities" (*Good News Bible*) produced by a Christlike character. Christian character is the spiritual harvest of goodwill and good deeds, acts of right-doing and acts of kindness that benefit others.

Christianity Found Hard, but Not Tried
Paul's prayer in Philippians 1:3-11 highlights the centrality of the gospel for the development of stable, godly character. Christian character, whether lived within the secular environment of the marketplace or the framework of church ministry, must stem from a shared commitment to the cause of Christ.

* Does my life give evidence that I live for something greater than myself? Something worthy, something true?
* Does my life give evidence that I am trusting in an all-powerful, sovereign God? Or am I trusting in my own ability to "fix" my life or the life of the church?
* What is the evidence that my life is characterized by the knowledge and wisdom of God?

- Do the habits of my mind and life show that I am concerned for the welfare of the church's task of proclaiming the gospel?
- Does my commitment to the gospel produce acts of kindness, love, and humility?

If our lives are focused on God's kingdom, the pressures that build tension will be overshadowed by the power of the good news. Spirit-filled Christian character is built on the Word of God and tested by our mutual partnership in the gospel. It creates an environment for spiritual maturity and church growth.

G.K. Chesterton fittingly remarked, "It is not that Christianity has been tried and found wanting, but that it has been found hard and not tried."[3]

Endnotes

[1] Quoted in Gerald F. Hawthorne, *Word Biblical Commentary,* Vol. 43, *Philippians* (Waco, TX: Word, 1983), 26.

[2] The NIV renders the words *pase aisthesei* as "depth of insight." This leaves the idea vague. Insight into what? Literally, the Greek intimates "in all—or extensive — perception." This is the only occurrence of *aisthesei* in the New Testament, although it is found in the Greek translation of Proverbs (1:4, 7, 22; 3:20; 5:2). The idea in secular Greek is "common sense." Thus Paul probably means "depth of insight into making the best moral choices possible." See Hawthorne, 26-27.

[3] Quoted in J.I. Packer, *A Quest for Godliness: The Puritan Vision of the Christian Life* (Wheaton, IL: Crossway, 1990), 308.

CHAPTER 3

The Measure of a Meaningful Life

Philippians 1:12-26

GEORGE STOWELL, FOUNDER OF THE Industrial Youth Center of Bridgeport, Connecticut, and I were driving through the one of the city's more poverty-stricken sections. For most of my life, I was a suburbanite, and I could find inner-city life a bit disturbing. I purposely spent time with George, who runs an inner-city youth ministry, because I needed to get over that discomfort. I need to learn how the Christian life can affect those living in the despair of hope.

George pointed to a street corner where drugs are sold. He pointed out another corner where a teenager was gunned to death just the day before. I wondered out loud at all the people hanging out on the street corners.

"The same people seem always to be on the same corners every time we drive through," I commented. "Why do they just stand around doing nothing?"

"They have nothing to live for," George answered. "Hope is gone. Life itself has no meaning for them."

"How sad!" I said. "We've attempted so many programs and government-sponsored solutions, but none of them seems to work."

George has ministered among inner-city people for many years. He knows their despair—especially the despair the kids feel.

"I try in some small way to give them a little hope," George said. "I try to give them a hope that does not change because of who's in political office or whether there's money for temporal programs."

George continued. "That's a good deal of the problem. Most solutions stem from temporal concepts, ideas, or principles. These people need something beyond that, something eternal. The gospel is the only hope that can lift them *above*—not necessarily *out of*—this environment. Temporal solutions to such despairing situations ought to be sought. But none addresses the real human need for finding meaning in life. The gospel and a person's relationship to Jesus Christ is where such meaning is found. I've seen some of these kids find that meaning."

Christians, on the other hand, do not have to search long for a meaningful life. We have the measuring stick for such life in the gospel and in the person of Jesus Christ. Ironically, it was from Paul's unjust confinement while under house arrest that we discover the measure of a meaningful life. In Philippians 1:12-26, the incarcerated apostle offers us the method for measuring a meaningful life, shows us the way to participate and grow in this meaningful life and points out where God intends us to find the joy of a meaningful life.

Our Lives Are Measured by a Meaningful Purpose

"The real paradox of our time," someone has remarked, "is not poverty in plenty, but unhappiness in the pursuit of pleasure." Today there are more distractions from boredom than at any other time in history. Yet Malcolm Muggeridge comments:

> We have everything that we want materially, and it ought to make us happy, but for some reason it doesn't. It should be the case that...where all these material things are most available, where the pursuit of happiness is most ardently undertaken should also be the place where human beings are most happy...In fact, it's not so. Something has gone wrong. It hasn't worked.[1]

Why hasn't it worked? Why are masses of people, especially youth and young adults, so bored, aimless and even apathetic about life? Our culture—our media, our educators, our politicians, our technological advancements—cannot give the human heart ultimate purpose and meaning. Every person longs for a reason, a purpose for living. We tend, however, to draw our meaning from things and people that are earthly, transitory, susceptible to change and decay. What is lacking? Lacking is a purpose that raises us above the disenchantment and decay of our culture.

The Oscar-winning classic, *Chariots of Fire,* illustrates the search for meaning through the lives of two runners destined for Olympic gold medals, Harold Abrams and Eric Liddell. Abrams dreamed of being the fastest runner in the world. Liddell, a missionary's kid from China, dreamed of following in his parents' footsteps. He was caught up in preaching and preparing for his missionary service in China.

Harold Abrams wins his race. He has accomplished all he ever wanted to do. Instead of satisfaction, however, he finds his life empty, bankrupt. Meanwhile, Liddell is confronted by his sister. She is concerned that the running will distract him from his call to China.

"I know that God has made me for China," Liddell assures his sister. "But He has also made me fast. And when I run, I feel His pleasure."

What is the difference between these two men? Abrams had nothing but his win for pleasure. Once he won, he was without a goal. Eric Liddell had his run. But once it was finished, he had China. After China, he had heaven. (Liddell died a missionary martyr in China.) Eric Liddell knew *why* he was created, and *that* was his pleasure. He was created for a purpose—the glory and service of God.

Rising above Adversity

The apostle Paul astounds us by his ability to cope with and rise above adversity. Did Paul have some special endowment of power? Yes. Is this power available for us? Yes again. The power for Paul's life was drawn from a supernatural Source *and* a worthy cause: the Person of Christ and the ministry of the gospel. Herein lies his secret for a meaningful life.

Amid false accusations and from his confining circumstances, Paul reassures the Philippians:

> *My circumstances have turned out for the progress of the gospel rather than hindering it. As a result of my chains, my participation in the cause of Christ has become apparent among the entire praetorium guard and to everyone else.* (1:12-13, author's translation)

Paul is saying, "Don't mind the incarceration. Look, even

these chains have become links in the advance of the gospel."

Paul's positive attitude and confidence toward life and the gospel are not mere altruism. He knows what is at stake. It was rumored that since the great apostle could be imprisoned, the gospel must be impotent, perhaps even untrue.

Once the significance of the gospel is removed or in doubt as the central purpose for an individual's life, both nonbelievers and the Church suffer. Those without Christ will disregard the seriousness of the gospel's message, thus forfeiting true life and the forgiveness of sins. The Church can be threatened by division, disarray and a lack of power.

Looking for an Anchor

Non-Christians want to know if the gospel we proclaim is true and meaningful. People are seeking an anchor for their lives—something that will not move, decay or change. They are looking for something worthy of their trust. One skeptic and critic chides the Church:

> The world expects of Christians that they will raise their voices so loudly and clearly…that not even the simplest man can have the slightest doubt about what they are saying. Further, the world expects of Christians that they will eschew all fuzzy abstractions and plant themselves squarely in front of the bloody face of history. We stand in need of folk who have determined to speak directly and unmistakably and, come what may, to stand by what they have said.[2]

The world wants to know if we take the gospel seriously. They want to know if the gospel is able to provide the meaning they long for.

Our confidence in the gospel will build confidence in those who follow our lead. Paul adds, "Also, as a result of my chains, most of the brethren have confidence in the Lord, so that they have far more courage to speak the gospel without fear" (1:14, author's translation). Christians are to know that the cause of Christ is worth pursuing and proclaiming—whatever the adversity (Romans 8:31-39). Such conviction will dissolve the doubts of those who question the gospel's power.

Who follows in our footsteps? Friends, workmates, spouses, children, Christian brothers and sisters. Each of us is in a singular place to influence someone else's life. What kind of influence will it be? We can demonstrate a life anchored on the Solid Rock, Christ Jesus. Or we can give in to the whims of hardship. When the gospel is our central concern, we will be focused. We will have meaning in life and we will show others how to have meaningful lives.

Our Sanctification Is Measured by Our Motives

Special interest groups proliferate on the North American scene. Each demands certain inalienable rights. When those rights clash with some other group's rights, tension mounts and there is rivalry. This special interest mentality has seeped into the Church. Its effect on the progress of the gospel has been devastating.

We see the special interest mentality in our church growth slogans. An example: "This church is not your father's church" (a take-off on the old commercial, "This is not your father's Oldsmobile"). The implication is that we are living in a modern world, and our ways of doing church must reflect contemporary styles. Otherwise we shall not reach the baby boomers—the power brokers who determine a church's growth, stagnation or decline.

Christian sanctification has become a venture in privatized religion. Perhaps this is where the fault lies in our thinking. Christians are rather comfortable seeking their own personal interests (translate that "special interests") both inside and outside the church. But somehow the gift of God's meaningful life eludes them. Once a person discovers true life in the gospel, he or she cannot sustain contentment and joy without persevering in the faith (Romans 5:1-5). Sanctification, both the decision to grow in Christ and the process of such growth, must accompany one's discovery of the gospel, God's highest purpose.

One would almost think that our sanctification is the process whereby we become more comfortable "in the world" as Christians. This, however, is quite contrary to biblical sanctification and Christian spirituality. Sanctification is two-edged. On the one hand, it is the process by which we are further severed from the world. On the other hand, our sanctification must also move us closer to God's will and purpose. We must make a clear-cut decision to bring ourselves before God. We must renounce motives that promote our self-interests. We must clothe ourselves with attitudes that promote the welfare of others. A.B. Simpson put it this way: "The Holy Spirit leads us to a deeper separation, not only from evil but from the earthly, lifting us into a supernatural life."[3]

Two Very Different Motives
In Philippians 1:15-17, Paul depicts two different motivations for participating in the gospel:

> *It is true that some preach Christ out of envy and rivalry, but others out of goodwill. The latter do so in love, knowing that I am put here for the defense of the gospel. The former preach Christ out of selfish ambition, not sincerely, supposing that they can stir up trouble for me while I am in chains.*

Both groups were participating in the proclamation of the gospel. To the outsider, both groups appeared equally dedicated. One group, however, was motivated by a desire to "get on Paul's nerves" and perhaps portray him as a dud-apostle. ("Would God permit a mighty man—especially a God-appointed apostle—to remain month after month under house arrest?") The other group was motivated by love. Those in that group understood that Paul was in prison precisely because he was defending the gospel. Therefore, they would carry on faithfully in his stead.

Don't overlook the importance of the context. Paul was subtly speaking to the "in-house" rivalry in Philippi (2:3-4; 4:2). His letter was to correct the status-seeking rivalry within the congregation and to put the church back on its joyful course of participation in the gospel. Paul is indicating what should motivate us and how to handle our own attitudes toward the motives of others.

What Motivates Us Is Important

What motivates us will determine both our joy in this life and our recompense at the judgment seat of Christ (2 Corinthians 5:9-10). Our personal investment in the activities of the church should not cause a rivalry within the congregation or among other churches. Our motivation should stem from a sincere love for the truth (Philippians 1:18) and a sincere love for others (2:1-4).

Paul's second concern—guarding our own motives—is revealed in his confidence of deliverance: "I know that through your prayers and the help given by the Spirit of Jesus Christ, what has happened to me will turn out for my deliverance" (1:19). This is one of those texts where we respond to the obvious and miss the significant. Obviously Paul longs for release from prison. It is a natural, human reaction. But we overlook this question: *Why* would Paul's adversity *result* in his "deliverance"?

Is Paul really saying he expected to be released from prison? The word translated *deliverance* can also mean *salvation*. Many scholars have concluded that Paul was indeed released from this imprisonment. He himself expected it (1:24-26). But here he may not have been speaking of deliverance from his chains. Rather, he may be referring to his salvation when he stands before the judgment seat of Christ (2 Corinthians 5:10).[4]

Paul rhetorically asks, "What does this imprisonment matter?" And he goes on: "The important thing is that in every way, whether from false motives or true, Christ is preached. And because of this I rejoice. Yes, and I will continue to rejoice" (1:18). He is saying in effect, "Am I in despair over being a prisoner of Rome? Am I dismayed over the pretense of my opponents? Not at all! The gospel is still advancing, and in *this* I rejoice." Paul's concern is his relationship to the gospel, and thus his sanctification. This is his point:

> *I eagerly expect and hope that I will in no way be ashamed, but will have sufficient courage so that now as always Christ will be exalted in my body, whether by life or by death.* (1:20)

Adversity Is a Part of the Sanctifying Process

Elsewhere Paul alludes to how adversity is a part of the sanctifying process that produces perseverance:

> *Not only so, but we also rejoice in our sufferings, because we know that suffering produces perseverance; perseverance, character; and character, hope. And hope does not disappoint us, because God has poured out his love into our hearts by the Holy Spirit, whom he has*

given us. (Romans 5:3-5)

The apostle John further reminds us that our ultimate motivation comes from God's final word on our lives:

Now, dear children, continue in him, so that when he appears we may be confident and unashamed before him at his coming. (1 John 2:28)

Surely Paul does not intend for us to be tolerant of heresy. Elsewhere he attacks it with a vengeance (Galatians 1:6-10; Colossians 2:16-23; Philippians 3:1-3). But Paul will not be ashamed at the Lord's coming because he has not demonstrated a vindictive attitude toward those who have belittled his ministry. He has been able to endure the "bad press" and the adversity. Why? Because his ultimate motivation for life is the progress of the gospel, not his pride or self-preservation. He wants to engender in the Philippian believers the same wholesome attitude.

Our sanctification is dependent on the power of the Spirit and the prayers of the saints. Paul says: "I know that through your prayers and the help given by the Spirit of Jesus Christ, what has happened to me will turn out for my deliverance" (1:19). Our lives, whether our daily sanctification or our ultimate place before God's judgment seat (Romans 14:10-12; 1 Corinthians 3:10-15), are dependent upon both the Spirit and the Church. For our motivation we cry out to the Spirit for help in our weaknesses. We joyfully show our dependence on the prayers of fellow believers. When our motives stem from goodwill, we enrich our sanctification and thus increase our joy (Philippians 1:18; 4:4).

Our Joy Is Measured by Our Love for the Church
Former American President John F. Kennedy rallied a

nation with his famous, "Ask not what your country can do for you; ask what you can do for your country." Martin Luther King, Jr., united the civil rights movement by his words, "I have a dream." Catchy phrases and calculated sound bites are a part of our North American psyche. They can have an impact that far exceeds their brevity. Unlike these calls for the greater good of others, we find a more privatized, self-centered attitude current today.

Modern marketing slogans amplify this attitude. A fast-food restaurant advises us: "You deserve a break today." An automaker informs us that their cars "change everything." A soft drink imparts friendship: "You're a part of me!" A car ad supplies intimacy: "I love what you do for me." A hamburger chain offers us choices: "Have it your way."

In 1:21 Paul delivers a notable slogan: "To me, to live is Christ and to die is gain." It is a verse nearly all seasoned Christians can quote. Throughout Church history it has been a motivating biblical affirmation. But our overemphasis on the individual has distorted its intended meaning. To hear it as a personal, deeper life one-liner is to hear it apart from its context.

Paul is summarizing the meaning of human existence. In effect he is saying, "Life is summarized in one word: Christ. Christ is the Definer and the Sustainer of my existence." We must hear this, not as Christian rhetoric for a privatized faith, but within the context of sanctification.

> *If I am to go on living in the body, this will mean fruitful labor for me. Yet what shall I choose? I do not know! I am torn between the two: I desire to depart and be with Christ, which is better by far; but it is more necessary for you that I remain in the body.* (1:22-24)

Christlikeness Should Mean Commitment to a Church

The chairman of my church board made what I consider a very appropriate statement. "When someone grows in sanctification," he said, "and develops more into the image of Christ, that person should equally grow in his or her commitment to the church."[5] That is Paul's point exactly!

Certainly the outside pressures of life (being "torn" or "hard-pressed")[6] can squeeze us. They can make it difficult to persevere in the faith. The tendency, when we face adversity or hardship, is to retreat inward—a survival mentality takes over. This is potentially damaging for the Church and can hinder the advance of the gospel. When we realize that Christ is our life (1:21), the accompanying truth is that our lives exist for the benefit of the church. This flies in the face of our privatizing tendency.

> *Convinced of this, I know that I will remain, and I will continue with all of you for your progress and joy in the faith, so that through my being with you again your joy in Christ Jesus will overflow on account of me.* (1:25-26)

Paul has expressed joy that the gospel was indeed progressing despite the preachers of contempt (1:18). He has reflected on his position before God—"I eagerly expect and hope that I will in no way be ashamed" (1:20). Now Paul applies his extraordinary life to the benefit and progress of the church (1:26). Our joy will be to follow his lead. We are to be people of worthy purpose (the progress of the gospel), people of honorable motivation and people in love with the Church.

How Is My Impact?

A friend once made the observation that it seems many

church leaders tend to put their ministry careers above the good of the church. I must confess that was once my attitude.

Frequently the question is asked of aspiring pastors and missionaries, "Are you making decisions for your life with the Church's needs in mind?" "Are you making life decisions in light of what is best for Christ and His Church?" Although these questions are highly relevant for future church workers, they apply as well to every Christian.

Paul is beckoning each of us to make our lives extraordinary, not for ourselves and our personal needs and aspirations and certainly not at the expense of the Church. We are to do it for the progress of the gospel and the building up of the Church.

The psalmist cries out: "Save me, O God, for the waters have come up to my neck" (Psalm 69:1). Listen as he pours out his supplication to God:

> *You know my folly, O God;*
> > *my guilt is not hidden from you.*
> *May those who hope in you not be disgraced*
> *because of me,*
> *O Lord, the LORD Almighty;*
> > *may those who seek you not be put to shame*
> > *because of me,*
> > *O God of Israel.*
> *For I endure scorn for your sake,*
> > *and shame covers my face.*
> *I am a stranger to my brothers, an alien to my own*
> *mother's sons;*
> > *for zeal for your house consumes me,*
> > *and the insults of those who insult you fall*
> *on me.* (Psalm 69:5-9)

We must learn not to measure our lives by the "scorn" and "shame" that, like our Master, we are sometimes called to endure. The important questions are these: *How clearly can God be seen in my life? Is my life impacting positively on others?* When you measure up to those two questions, you will indeed have a meaningful life.

Endnotes
[1] Geoffrey Barlow, ed., *Vintage Muggeridge: Religion and Society* (Grand Rapids, MI: Eerdmans, 1985), 12.

[2] Albert Camus, quoted in Os Guinness, *The Dust of Death: A Critique of the Counter Culture* (Downers Grove, IL: InterVarsity, 1973), 364.

[3] Keith M. Bailey, ed., *The Best of A.B. Simpson,* (Camp Hill, PA: Christian Publications, 1987), 53.

[4] For a more detailed explanation of this interpretation, see Moises Silva, *Philippians* (Chicago:, IL Moody Press, 1988), 76-79.

[5] Thanks, Scott! An insightful word on church growth. Perhaps more Christians *like* yourself will come to realize this important principle.

[6] Elsewhere the word translated "torn" (NIV) or "in a strait" (KJV) is used to describe ill health (Luke 4:38), outward physical pressure (Luke 8:45) and inward spiritual pressure (Luke 12:50).

CHAPTER 4

In the Arena:
Christ versus Caesar
Philippians 1:27-30

⸎

W OODY ALLEN ONCE QUIPPED, "IT'S NOT that I am afraid to die. I just don't want to be there when it happens." Often Christians can take a similar attitude toward spiritual growth.

"It's not that I am afraid of spiritual growth," they say. "I just don't want to be there when it happens."

H.G. Wells once called Buddhism the "best religion." But he admitted it could only flourish in a warm climate.[1] Wells was not poking fun at Buddhism. He was commenting on Westerners' preference for comfort. Our modern version of Christianity is also unfavorably disposed toward discomfort. But any theme that gets as much space in the Scripture as suffering does should have our careful, reverent attention.

Suffering is no more avoidable than breathing. But let's face it. Today we view life through the lenses of comfort, personal rights and material affluence. Our culture is collapsing under the weight of a thousand rights and needs. Meanwhile, that same weight has become a millstone around the neck of Christian spirituality and those involved in gospel proclamation.

Our churches are filled with disappointed, disillusioned Christians. Many float from church to church, from one self-help book to another, from one get-healed-quick guru to another. They search for the "power" that will release their pain and unleash their happiness. The problem is not the gospel or the power of God's Word. The problem is our preference for comfort.

Modern Christians are more apt to shrink spiritually than to grow. In his book, *New Rules,* Daniel Yankelovich observes:

> You are not the sum total of your desires. You do not consist of an aggregate of needs, and your inner growth is not a matter of fulfilling all your potentials. By concentrating day and night on your feelings, potentials, needs, wants and desires, and by learning to assert them more freely, you do not become a freer, more spontaneous, more creative self; you become a narrower, more self-centered, more isolated one. You do not grow, you shrink.[2]

A Call to Comfort, the Call to Suffer

Much of our problem rests in our inability to reconcile our culture's call to comfort with the biblical texts calling us to suffer. And that's the scandal of contemporary Christian life.

We have a generation of Christians who cannot say with Aleksandr Solzhenitsyn, "Praise God for this prison." They cannot identify with Dietrich Bonhoeffer's conviction, "When Christ calls a man, He bids him come and die." They cannot understand the depths of A.W. Tozer's comment, "It is doubtful whether God can bless a man greatly until He has hurt him deeply."

The Bible, I fear, is much closer to Solzhenitsyn, Bonhoeffer and Tozer than we like to think.

We come in Philippians 1:27-30 to a disturbing text. The apostle not only exhorts us to walk worthy of the gospel. He also informs us that suffering is a gift of God—and is to be expected. This confronts us like a dreaded nightmare.

Philippians 1:27 begins a section that ends at Philippians 3:21. In his opening statement, Paul calls for a deepened commitment to the gospel, which necessitates our continued sanctification.[3] Paul turns our attention to the process of sanctification by answering the following questions:

- How do we walk worthy of the gospel? (1:27-30)
- How do we function as a Christian community? (2:1-30)
- How do we grasp the power of the cross and the resurrection? (3:1-21)

Our text answers the first question:

> *Whatever happens, conduct yourselves in a manner worthy of the gospel of Christ. Then, whether I come and see you or only hear about you in my absence, I will know that you stand firm in one spirit, contending as one man for the faith of the gospel without being frightened in any way by those who oppose you. This is a sign to them that they will be destroyed, but that you will be saved—and that by God. For it has been*

*granted to you on behalf of Christ not only to
believe on him, but also to suffer for him,
since you are going through the same struggle you saw I had, and now hear that I still
have. (1:27-30)*

Christian Spirituality Is Fought in Caesar's Arena
How do Christians live in Caesar's arena? Christians have
always struggled with living in two worlds at the same time.
Paul's answer: "Whatever happens, conduct yourselves in a
manner worthy of the gospel of Christ." The phrase *conduct
yourselves* would have produced an instant jolt. Literally,
the text says "conduct yourselves *as worthy citizens.*" It is
the Greek word *politeuesthe,* in which our English word
politics is recognizable. Although our citizenship is in
heaven (3:20), we must conduct our heavenly citizenship as
earthly pilgrims. Our feet get dirty from the dust of the
earth, but our hearts and minds absorb the glories of heaven.
Paul places the arena of our sanctification, our spiritual
growth, our heavenly pilgrimage, within an earthly realm:
Caesar's arena—of all places!

Joy Amid Suffering
There is an irony in Paul's letter to the Philippian congregation. His own circumstance is one of suffering (he's under
house arrest!). Yet Paul continually speaks of joy throughout the letter. And he calls the Christian community to share
in that joy. The latter part of our immediate context refers to
suffering (1:28ff.). One wonders how suffering and joy can
be part of the same oxygen that fills the lungs of a healthy
Christian. Joy we like. Suffering we can tolerate if it's in
athletics, but not in our walk with Christ!

The reason Christian suffering is a logical outwork-
ing of our relationship with Christ is that we are to be
conformed to Christ and not to this world. As we are being

sanctified, as we are growing in Christlikeness, we will always be at odds with this world. Thus we will always have a measure of suffering in our lives.

Paul is attempting to help the Christian community in Philippi relate their faith to their earthly existence. The King James Version turns this text, "Only let your conversation be as it becometh the gospel of Christ." This "conversation" is not merely words from our mouths but how we as Christians "converse" with this world—this culture. Paul's use of the word *gospel* suggests how we are to do this.

We are accustomed to the term *gospel* in a church or religious setting. For us the term carries a wide range of connotations: the Scripture, preaching, a Bible book, something that is true, a type of music, salvation, redemption, forgiveness, the cross—the list is long. Citizens of the Roman Empire, however, heard something else.

Throughout the Roman Empire the word *gospel* carried citizenship dynamics. When Caesar celebrated a birthday, the whole empire acclaimed the "gospel" of the Caesar. The anniversary of his accession to the throne was also celebrated empire-wide as "gospel." When Roman citizens heard the term *gospel,* they thought of the emperor who gave the empire stability, leadership and welfare. This is significant to the Philippian context.[4]

Welcome to "Little Italy"!
Philippi had acquired the nickname "Little Italy." To be a citizen of Philippi was tantamount to enjoying the full rights and privileges conferred on those who lived in Rome, the Imperial City. The citizens of Philippi were among the most loyal celebrators of the "gospel of Caesar." In this particular Roman colony, more than anywhere else, there was a tendency to flatter the Caesar with divine titles and honors. In essence, the Caesar was celebrated as the matrix for life, their "gospel."

Paul turns this whole concept on its head. Now the Christian citizens of Philippi were to live, not worthy of the gospel of Caesar, but worthy of the gospel of Christ. Jesus Christ provides the new matrix for life. The definition of our stability and well-being comes not from Rome (or any earthly government). It comes not from culture or from any earthly ruler, but from our heavenly Emperor, the Lord Jesus Christ.

It is legitimate to long for comfort and the absence of pain. Our momentary, light afflictions accentuate the future weight of glory where earthly suffering and hardship are no longer (2 Corinthians 4:16-5:10). But now we are aliens in a foreign land. As the songwriter puts it, "This world is not my home." The first step in reconciling our earthly afflictions and our heavenly longing for comfort is to understand that *Caesar and Christ met in the arena and Christ won.* The Christian community trusts not in any earthly benefactor but in the heavenly King, the Lord Jesus. We celebrate the gospel of Christ. Thus we are to walk worthy of our heavenly citizenship.

Christian Spirituality Is Sustained in the Arena of Community

Two vital aspects of sanctification are either neglected or too easily forgotten: the role of the Christian community and the role of suffering. Let's turn our attention to the first, the role of the Christian community.

The command is, "Conduct yourselves in a manner worthy of the gospel of Christ." How can we do this? Paul says we cannot do it alone. As earthly pilgrims with heavenly citizenship and gospel responsibility, we must have the sustaining help of our Christian family. We must make a mutual commitment to our church fellowship. He speaks of their "stand[ing] firm in one spirit, contending as one man for the faith of the gospel."

Earlier, in 1:19-25, Paul testified that his sanctification was intimately linked to the community of faith. Now he shows the same link between *our* sanctification and the Christian community. On the one hand, the Christian community is to be like soldiers "stand[ing] firm" at their posts, resisting the pressures of attack, refusing to leave their comrades to defend themselves (1 Corinthians 16:13; Galatians 5:1; Ephesians 6:10-18; Philippians 4:1).

On the other hand, the Christian community is also like an athletic team. Putting aside their differences, "contending as one man" (literally, "one soul"), they join their talents, gifts and determination to win the contest—together.

Our community of faith is to be a place of refuge and a place of strength. Here lies the *second step* in reconciling our heavenly residence to our earthly pilgrimage: *The Christian community, under the power of the Holy Spirit, provides the support and solidarity that each person needs to persevere under the pressures of opposition, hardship or pain.*

We believers are scattered throughout the countryside and in towns and cities. We live in condos, apartments and split-level homes. But we must think of our local church as a community under one roof, with one purpose and ruled by one King (Ephesians 4:1-6). It is in the context of our worshipping community—our local congregation—that Paul says we gain strength, perseverance and spiritual growth. Living in the context of community adds strength to the individual parts. It also enables each member to experience the disciplines of life.

There Are Negatives to Community
Think about what happens when we live within a community. In reality there will be a certain amount of pain:

- the clash of egos
- the contest for personal rights
- the disappointment of not getting our own way
- public embarrassment and injured pride
- conflicting needs and competing self-interests
- finding that deeply held convictions aren't the measure of reality—*or even of spirituality*

Community is a place where our reflexes and responses are tested. This testing, in turn, develops strength of character. Jean Vanier reminds us:

> A community is not just a place where people live under the same roof; that is a lodging house or a hotel. Nor is a community a work-team. Even less is it a nest of vipers. It is a place where everyone—or let us be realistic, the majority—is emerging from the shadows of egocentricity in the light of real love.[5]

No wonder Christian spirituality is often divorced from a sense of community. It is hard to "work things out." No one likes to surrender his or her ego. Sometimes we are like family members who separate themselves from the family rather than face up to their own self-centeredness or egotistic claims to personal rights.

Not infrequently Christians go the easy route and run from their fellowship. In doing so they forfeit the sanctification that God works through our relationship to the church. The church community is God's means of granting perseverance, joy and hope (Romans 15:1-13). Thus our sanctification is *sustained* in the arena of the church, our worshipping community of faith.

Christian Spirituality Is Nourished in the Arena of Affliction

Like C.S. Lewis in *The Problem of Pain,* if it were not for my backache, I could sit longer at my computer and write more clearly on the subject of Christian suffering. How does a person raised in affluence and taught to expect prosperity relate to the fact of suffering? Worse, how does he or she relate to the Christian *call* to suffering? I write under no illusion. I too wish for ease and comfort.

Paul could not be more bold or clear:

> *Conduct yourselves in a manner worthy of the gospel...Stand firm...without being frightened in any way by those who oppose you...For it has been granted to you on behalf of Christ not only to believe on him, but also to suffer for him, since you are going through the same struggle you saw I had, and now hear that I still have.* (Philippians 1:27-30)

The Scripture is replete with references to Christian suffering:

> "[Jesus said to His disciples,] *'I have told you these things, so that in me you may have peace. In this world you will have trouble. But take heart! I have overcome the world'."* (John 16:33)

> "*Then* [Paul and Barnabas] *returned to Lystra, Iconium and Antioch, strengthening the disciples and encouraging them to remain true to the faith. 'We must go through*

many hardships to enter the kingdom of God,' they said." (Acts 14:21-22)

"Now if we are children, then we are heirs— heirs of God and co-heirs with Christ, if indeed we share in his sufferings in order that we may also share in his glory...I consider that our present sufferings are not worth comparing with the glory that will be revealed in us." (Romans 8:17-18; see also 8:28-30)

"For our light and momentary troubles are achieving for us an eternal glory that far outweighs them all." (2 Corinthians 4:17; see also 4:7-12)

"We sent Timothy, who is our brother and God's fellow worker in spreading the gospel of Christ, to strengthen and encourage you in your faith, so that no one would be unsettled by these trials. You know quite well that we were destined for them." (1 Thessalonians 3:2-3)

"Of this gospel I was appointed a herald and an apostle and a teacher. That is why I am suffering as I am. Yet I am not ashamed, because I know whom I have believed, and am convinced that he is able to guard what I have entrusted to him for that day." (2 Timothy 1:11-12)

"Consider it pure joy, my brothers, whenever you face trials of many kinds, because you

> *know that the testing of your faith develops perseverance."* (James 1:2-3)

> *"Dear friends, do not be surprised at the painful trial you are suffering, as though something strange were happening to you. But rejoice that you participate in the sufferings of Christ, so that you may be overjoyed when his glory is revealed."* (1 Peter 4:12-13; see also 2:18-23)

The list could be much, much longer.

Don't Take the Politicians Too Seriously

Our difficulty in reconciling our faith to our earthly pilgrimage is illustrated by the political rhetoric we hear. Politicians are forever trying to attract our vote by alluding to other candidates who hinder *your* prosperity or *your* comfort. If we listen to them, we may be precariously near the proverbial slippery slope, thinking our Christian life is also in view. I find it incredible that Christians have sold their birthright for the mere stew of political rhetoric: "Today's generation earns less and has less than their parents' generation." No wonder we find it difficult to relate to "suffering" texts. Being sons and daughters of an age of affluence and comfort makes for an unbiblical view of spirituality. We must remember that God's sanctifying work will conform us to Christ, not to the world. And since the Christian life is often at odds with the world, suffering is unavoidable.

There seem to be two problems in applying "suffering" texts to contemporary Christians. The first, our Western world context is not perseverance amid persecution. It is rather perseverance amid pleasure. The second, our cited examples of suffering tend to be the "great Christians" of history with whom we find it hard to identify.

So what are we to do?

As dual citizens of heaven and our earthly culture of comfort, I suggest two principles for our pilgrimage here. Both are in light of the biblical call to suffer. The first stems from our culture; the second, from our Philippians text.

Principle One

First, *we must recognize that we are a people who lack discipline. Thus we should make some effort to live a more disciplined Christian faith.*

Michael Crichton's book *Jurassic Park* is a page turner. The author keeps his reader in the story through vivid images of prehistoric dinosaurs who have been reborn into the late twentieth century. Of course, the book's characters are fascinated by this creative venture—and the size of the creatures! Nevertheless, some doubt the Jurassic Park project is wise. The sharpest censure comes from the mathematician, summoned to review the park and give helpful suggestions and a positive confirmation of the project. His rebuke is very relevant to our discussion of suffering in an age of comfort.

The state-of-the-art dinosaur theme park had become a house of horrors. The reborn, giant reptiles were loosed to feed among the helpless humans. The mathematician, after encountering one of the hungry beasts, offered a rather scathing assessment, not of the result of one man's dream but of the cause of the nightmare they all were experiencing. Here is how he saw the problem:

> Most kinds of power require a substantial sacrifice by whoever wants the power. There is an apprenticeship, a discipline lasting many years. Whatever kind of power you want. President of a company. Black belt in karate. Spiritual guru. Whatever you seek,

you have to put in the time, the practice, the effort. You must give up a lot to get it. It has to be very important to you.

The mathematician goes on to rebuke the scientists because they had inherited their discoveries, their dreams, without long hard discipline. "You made progress very fast...There is no discipline lasting many decades."[6]

Born into Comfort

Let's face it. We inherited our faith in a context of comfort. Our forefathers were the ones who paid the price for our religious freedom and our prosperous churches. Now we build mega-churches and have multimillion dollar ministry budgets and an array of worship styles to fit every personality. Christianity has become a commodity. The problem is that since we have inherited so much, we forget that we, too, must have a measure of discipline in our Christian walk.

Suffering in an age of pleasure is God's instrument for conforming us to Christ. The points of physical or emotional pain, inward stress and disappointing failure are where God is attempting to instill discipline.

Suffering is a wake-up call from God. He is warning us that...

- we cannot succeed in the Christian walk by ourselves; we need our church
- we are fallible, humble creatures of dust; we are not self-sufficient
- our egos have strangled our hope and joy; surrendered wills are a requisite for spiritual growth
- we have acquiesced to our culture's level of creature comfort rather than to God's higher calling of Christlikeness.

Principle Two

I suggest a second principle important to our earthly pilgrimage: *We must recognize that our earthly existence is not a measure of who we are. Thus we must learn to allow God's tools of suffering to produce His grace in and through us.*

At the beginning of Paul's testimony (1:12ff) he admitted that some did not recognize his apostleship. They saw only a man, imprisoned, weak—certainly not the powerful, Spirit-anointed apostle of God. Paul's outward appearance—in part because of the hardship he had suffered—caused his opponents to deride him as a fraud and fool. Likewise those around us see our humanity, our hardship, our emotional stress. They conclude that we are either wrong to believe in God or simply foolish.

We are to know that our loyalty and perseverance lead us heavenward. Meanwhile unbelievers laugh at our faith, for they see our loyalty to Christ leading either to persecution or to absurdity. Nevertheless, we are to know that God grants us the gift of suffering. Suffering...

- produces perseverance, which in turn produces character (Romans 5:1-5)
- reveals our loyalty, whether to self or to Christ
- reminds us of our humanity, thus identifying us with those outside of Christ
- is a gift of God in order that through it His grace may be made sufficient (2 Corinthians 12:7-10)

The Costly Conclusion

The costliness of our faith is not taken seriously by those attuned to our pleasure-oriented society. This is at least one reason why Christians struggle with their faith. We are presented with a gospel that requires no cost and a God who demands nothing from us. We are offered a sanctification lacking the riches of church fellowship. We are estranged from costly grace. Dietrich Bonhoeffer reminds us:

> Cheap grace means grace sold on the market like cheapjack's wares...Grace without price; grace without cost. The essence of grace, we suppose, is that the account has been paid in advance; and because it has been paid, everything can be had for nothing. Since the cost is infinite, the possibilities of using and spending it are infinite.[7]

This man of God cautions us: "Cheap grace is the deadly enemy of our church. We are fighting today for costly grace."

When our faith conforms to our culture, the costliness of grace will fade. And with it, our joy, hope and perseverance. The gospel and our sanctification demand a commitment to our church fellowship. That is the context here. That is Paul's plea.

We are to be worthy citizens of the gospel. This is not a transient commitment but a permanent obligation to the welfare of our church fellowship. As worthy citizens we should develop and express our individual potentials, not in isolation but in cooperation with our Christian fellowship. As fellow pilgrims of the gospel we do not bear our struggles alone. They are shared by our fellowship of saints.

If we Christians are to persevere in the faith, we must face the tensions created by "living in the world." We must make Jesus the matrix, the center of our lives.

Endnotes
[1] A.W. Tozer, "About Hindrances" in *The Root of the Righteous* (Harrisburg, PA: Christian Publications, 1955),

129-131. See also his essay, "Uses of Suffering," 131-134.

[2] Daniel Yankelovich, *New Rules: Searching for Self-fulfillment in a World Turned Upside Down* (New York: Bantam, 1982), 239.

[3] Philippians 1:27 and 3:20, each bearing the "citizen" motif, function as bookends to a section highlighting the way a community of faith carries out the process of sanctification Paul touches on in 1:12-26.

[4] For a fuller discussion of the social setting and its significance for understanding this text, see M.R. Mulholland's essay, "Sociological Criticism," in David Alan Black and David S. Dockery, eds., *New Testament Criticism and Interpretation* (Grand Rapids, MI: Zondervan, 1991), 297-316.

[5] Quoted in James Bell, *Bridge over Troubled Waters: Ministry to Baby Boomers, a Generation Adrift* (Wheaton, IL: Victor Books, 1993), 137.

[6] Michael Crichton, *Jurassic Park* (New York: Ballantine Books, 1993), 306.

[7] Dietrich Bonhoeffer, *The Cost of Discipleship* (New York: Macmillan Publishing Co., 1976), 45.

CHAPTER 5

Getting Beyond the Sphere of Spending

Philippians 2:1-4

THE PEOPLE FOR THE AMERICAN WAY asked thousands of United States citizens what they thought had made their country great. One after another pointed to their rights and freedoms. "Individualism." "You can do whatever you want." "We really don't have any limits." Those were typical responses.[1]

But latent in those answers is a problem. Americans have experienced a major shift in how they think about rights and freedoms. There was a time when those individual liberties were derived from extrinsic, transcendent values that set moral limits and produced community responsibility. Today, individual freedoms are no longer related to a transcendent God and His expressed Word, the Bible. Now Americans define themselves, their rights and their freedoms by intrinsic, self-centered values.

Paul Vitz, a psychology professor at New York University, observed that Americans live in a nation of 260 million supreme beings. And each one, he says, is a jealous god.[2]

Mary Ann Glendon, a Harvard law professor, writes: "Converging with the language of psychotherapy, rights talk encourages our all-too-human tendency to place the self at the center of our moral universe."[3]

Americans have ignored the consequences of an expanding catalog of rights and personal liberties. And now they are feeling the impact such expansion has on personal responsibilities and, especially, on the general welfare. Look at the American court system. It is almost at gridlock with suits over rights.

Once again we are confronted with the consequences of an overly privatized, self-centered worldview. America dispenses rights and grants unlimited freedom. At the same time emotional trauma and impoverished self-worth are causing widespread despondency. This is the fallout of deriving rights from and seeking self-satisfaction within the private sphere.

This private sphere of unlimited moral boundaries detached from community responsibility has developed into a social cancer. As Os Guinness observes, it has become "the sphere of spending rather than earning, and of personal fulfillment rather than public obligation."[4] Maintaining a self-demanding list of needs and rights is an expensive habit. The self has an insatiable appetite. Other people no longer look upon Americans as victorious champions of freedom; they see them as spoiled brats.

The Church Is Little Better

When we turn to the Church, we must admit sadly that the Church's character and image are little better. The Church too has succumbed to the culture's ruinous fascination with rights, freedom and individualism. The Church too is using the private sphere to define its rights, its freedoms and what it is as a body of Christians. The Church also tends to function as if "self" is the center of the universe. How then can it expect to confront or change our society's narcissism or heal the wounds stemming from rival self-interests?

As Christians and as church people, our spirituality, our process of sanctification must be countercultural. We must learn not to indulge the private sphere where self is king. We must get beyond our preoccupation with our own well-being. We must restore the church community's health and vitality.

In Philippians 2:1-4, Paul once more confronts our privatized Christian faith. He offers solutions for rebuilding true, joyous Christian spirituality. This is a biblical spirituality that puts the emphasis on community responsibilities. It is a spirituality that cancels our culture's crowning of the self-life.

Restoring the Joy Side of Christian Life

Picture Philippians 1:27-30, the focus of our previous chapter, and Philippians 2:12-18, the focus of chapter 6, as adjoining rooms. Both contain furnishings we need for spiritual growth. Philippians 2:1-4 and 2:5-11 serve as *double doors,* allowing us free passage to these two important rooms. One room is the room of suffering (1:27-30), as we noted; the other is the room of steadfast obedience (2:12-18). One of the doors (2:5-11) is marked *The Imitation of Christ.* We will give that door attention in chapter 6. The other door (2:1-4) is marked *The Character of the Christian Community.* It will have our attention now.

"Make my joy complete," Paul says (2:2). It is a command. We must recall that Paul is writing while "in chains" under house arrest. Even so, he could abound in joy if he knew the Philippian congregation was living in humility and harmony. Disunity within the ranks and a spirit of rivalry had sapped their Spirit-given joy.[5] Paul's main concern is to bring harmony back to the Christian community and thus restore their joy—and his own.

A church (any church) centered on itself is in trouble. Paul endeavors to shift the Philippians' attention from themselves to Christ and His kingdom work. And he saw himself, suffering under house arrest in Rome, as an integral part of Christ's kingdom work. He would involve the Philippians in his ministry and get their attention off themselves. It would be a major step in restoring the health of the Philippian church.

Let us not neglect the broader context here. Suffering is a fact of life. As Paul puts it in 1:27-30, it is a gift of God granted to believers. Paul integrates 2:1-4 into what he has been saying about sanctification. Thus it is related to how the Church perseveres through hardship and affliction.

The apostle wants his readers to sense deeply the need for harmony and mutual concern within the Church body. He understands that when the self-life is crowned, perseverance and true joy will be in short supply. To restore the joy side of the Christian life, we must learn to live beyond and above the private sphere. The key to joyous spiritual growth amid adversity is to shift attention from self-interest to the needs of others.

Attitudes to Joy and Spiritual Growth
In 2:1 we discover the means for restoring—and sustaining—joyous spiritual growth. This discovery will enable the individual Christian to conform his or her character to the mind-set of Christ (2:5). Corporately for the Church, this discovery will return the Church to robust health.

First, there is the *encouragement from being united with Christ.* What does Paul mean by *encouragement?* Elsewhere he uses this word to motivate others to follow what he has written (cf. Romans 12:1; 15:30; 16:17; 1

Corinthians 1:10; 4:16; 16:15; Ephesians 4:1; Philippians 4:2; 1 Timothy 2:11-12; 5:14). The encouragement Paul offers is based on God's activity through Christ and the Church's relationship to that activity. He is saying, "Since I have encouraged you already in the first portion of this letter regarding your life in Christ, find joy in that encouragement." If we would see our joy restored, we need to find our life sustained by God's truth. We need to be captivated by Jesus Christ.

Second, there is the *consolation of love.*[6] We might assume Paul is speaking here of God's love. This particular word for *consolation,* however, is never used directly of God's love or comfort. Paul is rather referring to his affection toward the Philippians, an attitude obvious throughout the letter. This word means "to come alongside" or "to speak kindly" to another. Paul is pleading that if the Philippians have found strength and comfort in his exhortations, they too can fortify others in the same manner. To restore our own joyous spiritual growth, we must "come alongside" others in a kind and friendly manner, helping and sustaining them amid their hardships.

Third, Paul speaks of "fellowship of the Spirit." Our culture's values and society's mores did not create, nor do they sustain, the Church. Our fellowship, our *koinonia,* is created by God and sustained by His Spirit (2 Corinthians 13:14). The connotation of *fellowship* here must also include what Paul has indicated previously in the letter. In Philippians 1:5 and 1:7 he has already thanked them for their shared partnership in the gospel. Our joy is sustained by our participation in a fellowship—the Church—that is created by God's Spirit and sustained by a mutual commitment to the gospel.

Fourth, *affection and compassion.* We must ask, whose affection and whose compassion? Paul has already indicated that he longs to see the Philippian believers "with the affection of Christ Jesus" (1:8). We discover elsewhere that Paul uses the word *compassion* to indicate Christ's activity (Romans 12:1; 2 Corinthians 1:3). Therefore Paul seems to be saying, "If you have been touched by the compassion of Christ, think and act that same way toward your fellow Christians."

Transcendent Principles for Living above the Private Sphere

Americans once looked outside themselves for a common denominator that held life together. Now, as we noted earlier in this chapter, they are looking inward to the private sphere—the self. In order to be done with our society-driven narcissism and anxiety, we must have some measure of objectivity. Sanctification is not simply an inward inclination toward fuzzy concepts of altruism and self-denial. Our sanctification is linked to something greater than our own well-being.

Each of us is different. No one will debate that. Each of us has different needs. But for unity, harmony and mutual concern to exist, there must be some measure of objectivity. Paul lists three such principles.

We are to be *like-minded.* It is a frequent exhortation in the Pauline letters (cf. Romans 12:16; 15:5-6; 2 Corinthians 13:11; Philippians 4:2). But a "like-mind" for what? Each time Paul mentions like-mindedness, he refers to the welfare of fellow Christians and our shared interest in the gospel. He is not saying we must have conformity of thought. He *is* saying our attitude should evidence concern for the health of the Church and the increase of the gospel. That should be a common denominator marking every member of the Church.

We are to have *the same love.* Paul continues to plead for unity by defining how we exercise this "like-mind." Each Christian is called to imitate the sacrificial love demonstrated by Christ Jesus. John the apostle explains it clearly: "This is how we know what love is: Jesus Christ laid down his life for us. And we ought to lay down our lives for our brothers" (1 John 3:16; see also John 15:13). Something outside ourselves sets the standard for how we relate to fellow Christians. Christ's sacrificial love defines how we are to treat one another.

We are to be *in one spirit and purpose*. Literally Paul is saying we are to be "one-souled" or "soul-joined." Paul told the Corinthians that each member was important and needed (1 Corinthians 12, 14). Here he indicates that each member is intimately joined in mutual partnership through the Holy Spirit.

Our joyous spiritual growth and perseverance are dependent on a shared cause: our partnership in the gospel of Jesus Christ. Paul is exhorting the Philippians—and us— literally to "think about one thing." We are not to be consumed by the inner callings of the private sphere—the self. We are not to be distracted by culturally imposed expectations of freedom or standards of self-worth. Our attention is to be focused on one thing: the gospel. When we are intent on the gospel, we rise above the lures of our culture's self-fascination. The result is Spirit-given joy.

Developing Character That Transcends the Private Sphere
In Philippians 2:2 we have found some external common denominators for restoring joyous spiritual growth and strengthening our local fellowship. Now 2:3-4 suggest the type of character we will need in order to transcend the demands of our private sphere. We must bear in mind the issues at stake in Philippi: unity, mutual concern for the church and joyous participation in the gospel. We can expect, therefore, to find ways to shift attention away from ourselves and onto others.

> *Do nothing out of selfish ambition or vain
> conceit, but in humility consider others
> better than yourselves (2:3).*

"Selfish ambition" and "vain conceit" are characteristics expressed by those who arrogantly claim to know
best. Paul wrote to the Galatians to "not become conceited,
provoking and envying each other" (Galatians 5:26).
Elsewhere *envy* and *selfishness* are signs of division
(Philippians 1:15, 17). They are contrary to God's own character (1 John 4:7-9). Paul will later in this letter commend
Timothy for a quite opposite spirit (Philippians 2:21; see
also 1 Corinthians 10:24).

The welfare and health of the church are at stake.
Our motives are the issue. We are to operate on the basis of
humility. We are to regard others as more important than
ourselves. Only in this way will we maintain our faith and
endure hardship and the realities of "living in the world."
We must refuse to see ourselves as the center of the
universe.

> *Each of you should look not only to your own
> interests, but also to the interests of others
> (Philippians 2:4).*

How do we know if we are more interested in the
concerns of others than in our own? Paul offers us a test. We
know it when we are looking out for the interests of others.

There were certain ones in the Philippian congregation selfishly emphasizing their own needs without due
consideration for others. When everyone is looking out for
number one, we will not have the strength of character to
endure life's pressures. A fractured, partisan church cannot
be a source of strength or a sustaining place of refuge. The
corrective, as we will note in the next chapter, is to have the

mind of Christ (2:5). We are to imitate the One who placed the highest value on "pouring Himself out" for the interests of others.

Exchange Self for Christ

A medical missionary remarked: "If you plant for a year, plant rice. If you plant for a decade, plant trees. If you plant for a century, plant people."

We are preoccupied with how we relate to the *moment*—whether we are happy *now,* fulfilled and satisfied *now,* pain-free, problem-free *now.* We are not considering the long-term consequences of our fascination with self. We are planting seeds not calculated to produce a healthy, enduring, joyous Church. We are planting rice!

The Christian's present preoccupation with self-interest has dire consequences for the health and welfare of the Church. It also has consequences for the Church's mission. We are dangerously imitating the narcissism that runs unchecked throughout our society. We have exchanged the image of Christ for the image of Narcissus.

Narcissus was the mythical son of the Greek river god, Cephissus. Narcissus was distinguished for his beauty. His mother told him that he would have a long life provided he never looked upon his own features. But the temptation was too great. As Narcissus passed a pool of water, this handsome son of the river god gazed at his reflection. Immediately he became infatuated. He fell so deeply in love with his own image that he had room for no one else. And his life ended prematurely.

Greek mythology for sure. But the lesson is timeless. The charm of individualism has grown cancerous. In our own society our well-being itself is threatened.[7] This fascination with self and self-interest endangers a nation's freedoms. And when Christians express the same narcissism, the Church is put at risk and Christians are robbed of their joy.

It Is Hard to Overstate the Problem

In this age of consumerism and self-worship, people attend church not because God is worthy but because it is self-satisfying.[8] Whether saved or seekers, if they do not find the church self-satisfying, they look for one that will be. Or possibly they will lead to another religion that they think will be, or to the secular and pagan offerings of our materialistic age. This kind of privatized, self-centered world is at enmity with the gospel. It is contrary to true Christian spirituality.

I have hardly overstated the problems stemming from the culture of our day. Christians need to repent of their self-centeredness. We have allowed selfishness to define our existence. We appeal to the private sphere to measure our self-worth and to explain what the Church and God are to do *for us.* The gospel no longer judges us; we judge it. This is a far cry from Paul's exhortation in Philippians 2:1-4. Every phrase calls us to turn our attention away from ourselves and toward others. The tension between our seducement to cultural comfort and our call to God's intended design for sanctification compels us to answer difficult questions:

- What captivates you? Is it the world, or is it the truth of Christ Jesus?
- Do you purposefully find ways to encourage others?
- How are you strengthening your local church? Are you concerned for its welfare?
- Do you love others sacrificially?
- Do you sometimes (or regularly) put yourself ahead of others?
- Do you sometimes (or regularly) choose to look out for your personal interests to the neglect of the interests of others?
- Are you living for something greater than your own well-being?

Endnotes

[1] "Democracy's Next Generation," (Washington: People for the American Way, 1989), 14, 67-69.

[2] Peter J. Leithart, "The Politics of Emma's Hand," *First Things,* 51 (March 1995): 16-17.

[3] Mary Ann Glendon, *Rights Talk: The Impoverishment of Political Discourse* (New York, NY: Free, 1991), xi.

[4] Os Guinness, *The Gravedigger File* (Downers Grove, IL: InterVarsity, 1983), 82.

[5] Elsewhere in the letter Paul shares his joy or exhorts believers to share in his joy (1:4, 18, 25-26; 2:17-18; 3:1; 4:4).

[6] The New American Standard Bible at this point is preferred over the New International Version. See Gerald F. Hawthorne, *Word Biblical Commentary,* Vol. 43, *Philippians* (Waco, TX: Word, 1983), 64-67. The NASB is used for the remainder of 2:1.

[7] See Bellah, et. al., *Habits of the Heart: Individualism and Commitment in American Life* (New York, NY: Harper & Row, 1985), viii.

[8] See Douglas D. Webster, "Meeting Felt Needs" and "Transforming Felt Needs," in *Selling Jesus: What's Wrong with Marketing the Church* (Downers Grove, IL: InterVarsity, 1992), 74-114.

CHAPTER 6

Putting Jesus Back into Our Potential
Philippians 2:5-11

❦

TWO DECADES AGO *TIME MAGAZINE* ANNOUNCED God's funeral. The announcement was nothing new, of course. More than a century ago Friedrich Nietzsche had already eulogized God's passing. Since God is dead and "no new god lies as yet in the cradle and swaddling clothes," there is no alternative except to face up to our meaningless existence. Now modern man must "rise from the ashes of former values and ideals" and define his own potential and will its fulfillment.[1]

God's funeral wake has left us to ourselves. Fulfilling our own potential is now life's core occupation and our deepest need. Or so these secular, and sadly, too often, the religious pundits of pop culture would have us believe.

Evangelicals themselves have not totally escaped this frame of mind. Even if the evangelical community has not quite buried God, we certainly have tamed Him. We have refashioned Him into the image of an omnipotent

Friend or divine Psychologist who champions our full potential. This, in turn, has led to a new focus for measuring spirituality. Rather than for Christlikeness to be our goal, we now strive to reach "our full potential." This is the new aim of spiritual growth. Much that passes for evangelicalism today is only a disguised form of self-worship. God is "little more than a narcissistic projection of [our] own needs and desires."[2] We are preoccupied with self-fulfillment, not self-surrender.

Our Potential: Who Defines It?

The question is not whether we should seek our full potential. The question is, What *is* that potential? Who prescribes it for us? How do we know when we reach it?

Scripture defines that potential a bit differently than does our culture. The world pushes us to seek a potential that puts self at the center of our universe. The Bible declares that our potential is *discovered* in the Person of Jesus Christ, *measured* by Christlikeness and *pursued* through participation in the gospel. Conforming our lives to Christlikeness *is* seeking our potential. We call this the process of sanctification. Philippians 2:5-11 informs us how to define, aspire to and measure our full potential as Christians:

> *Your attitude should be the same as that of*
> *Christ Jesus:*
> >*Who, being in very nature God,*
> >>*did not consider equality with God*
> >>*something to be grasped,*
> >>*but made himself nothing,*
> >>*taking the very nature of a servant,*
> >>*being made in human likeness.*
> >*And being found in appearance as a man,*
> >>*he humbled himself*

and became obedient to death—
even death on a cross!
Therefore God exalted him to the highest place
and gave him the name
that is above every name,
that at the name of Jesus
every knee should bow,
in heaven and on earth
and under the earth,
and every tongue confess
that Jesus Christ is Lord,
to the glory of God the Father.

Putting the Mind of Christ Back into Our Potential

Pride and envy had taken its toll on the Philippian church. The congregation was ill. The antidote: a clear-cut decision to stop thinking of themselves and to focus on the needs of others (2:3-4). Living for something greater than our own well-being produces unity and harmony. It restores the health of the corporate body and produces spiritual growth and persevering joy among its individual members.

Throughout Church history there have been numerous interpretations of the term *sanctification* and as many suggested methods of achieving it. But those closest to biblical testimony recognize that our sanctification is a divine initiative whereby the Author of our salvation fills every facet of our beings with Himself.[3] This is exactly the direction Paul takes us in our text. He exhorts us to put Jesus Himself back into our sanctification.

The text indicates that our sanctification and the recovery of the Church's health are a community project: "Your attitude should be the same as that of Christ Jesus" (2:5). Do not let our English word *your* lull you into thinking Paul is merely addressing the individual. Of course, each individual must own the exhortation. But the *your* is inclusive. The emphasis is on the church as a whole. In order to heal the illness caused by selfishness, Paul exhorts the entire congregation to manifest Jesus' attitude—*His* thinking toward each other.

> *Think among yourself what Christ Jesus also thought. Let your bearing, your attitude, your disposition, your thoughts toward one another be what Jesus manifested*" (2:5, author's paraphrase).

In other words, put the mind of Christ back into your sanctification.

Philippians 2:6-11 both explains the mind of Christ and illustrates its application to our lives. The passage is known as the Christ-hymn. The words affirm for the Church His preexistence and His deity. The immediate issue for us, however, is to determine how this hymn text furthers Paul's overall purpose in his letter. How do these words slay the self-life and move us toward a healthier church and joyous spirituality?

The text affirms the deity of Jesus.[4] It is precisely because of His deity that His example is paramount for initiating and molding our sanctification. Philippians 2:6-11 *is* the Christian life. Jesus *is* the measure of our potential.

Having the Mind of Christ Means Adding to Our Potential

Likely you have heard the remark, "We no longer have heroes, we have celebrities." Have you considered the difference between a hero and a celebrity? Both are models for others to emulate. Each considers his or her potential. But there the similarities end.

You can tell celebrities because they gain from their celebrity status (whether power, wealth or fame). You can tell heroes because they lose something and others gain. Celebrities must be preoccupied with their own potential or they will lose their celebrity status. Heroes care not about themselves; their attention is on others.

Is it any wonder we have produced a very self-centered society? It is the price of modeling ourselves after celebrities. Imitating heroes, on the other hand, will diminish our narcissism (in and outside the church). It will enable us to gain once more a proper view of our potential and its fulfillment.

We do not have to search far for a hero to emulate. Jesus Himself is much more than an earthly hero. His attitude and actions provide us the highest possible model as we seek to fulfill our potential. "Being in very nature God, [he] did not consider equality with God something to be grasped, but made himself nothing, taking the very nature of a servant, being made in human likeness" (2:6-7).

Voluntarily Relinquish Your Rights

For Christians, the issue is not whether Jesus is God (we know He is!), but what He did as God. At first glance it looks as if Jesus conceded His position as God, laying aside His deity in order to take the place of a servant. But this is not quite Paul's idea.[5]

The word *himself* (2:7) is the direct object of the verb *made (nothing)* (*emptied,* NASB). In English, word order is important to communication. It is not as important in Greek. Greek writers positioned words in different places to help readers (who invariably read out loud) to hear a special point, a parallel thought or an emphasis. The Greek word order is "Himself He made nothing." If you read it aloud, you can almost hear it. The priority of *Him* gives the impression that Jesus voluntarily "made Himself nothing."

Here is the full sense of 2:6-7: "Jesus *voluntarily* made Himself nothing by becoming a servant, being made in the likeness of men, precisely *because* He was God" (author's translation and emphases). Jesus did not treat His equality with God as an excuse for selfishness. Rather, He turned away from His potential in glory precisely because it was to our advantage for Him to do so.

Add the Attribute of a Servant

The NIV translators used the words *made himself nothing* rather than the more familiar *emptied Himself* (NASB). Obviously they were attempting to circumvent what appears to be a vague statement about "emptying." Of what did Jesus "empty" Himself? He emptied Himself of His glory, His throne, His majesty, His almighty attributes of omnipotence and omnipresence, His supremacy. Such suggestions are hardly necessary. There is no real need to complete Paul's thought.

The idea of "emptying" (i.e., making Himself nothing) is simply that Jesus poured Himself out by becoming a servant. Jesus did not consider that being God gave Him the right to consider His own potential. Instead, He poured Himself out. He put Himself totally at the disposal of others (1 John 3:16; 2 Corinthians 8:9).

It is often perceived that the Christian life consists of "giving up," "forsaking," "abandoning," "relinquishing." Many look upon it as a life of subtractions. Although abandoning sinful activity or attitudes is necessary, perhaps we have portrayed the Christian life in reverse. If Jesus is the model for Christian living, then this portrait of Him in Philippians 2 indicates that Christian sanctification is not a process of subtraction—diminishing our potential—but of *adding to* our potential. The question is, *What are we to add?*

What Advantage Can I Give?

When Jesus became human He did not stop being God. As the One fully equal with the Father in deity and glory, He took on—He added—the attributes of a servant. Jesus, the King of glory, the almighty, powerful, everlasting true God, became a servant. It is not a question of what we should give up. Rather, how can we take what we have (our abilities, skills, talents, education, money, business acumen, creativity, even social status) to serve others for the sake of the gospel? For us to fulfill our potential, the question we must ask is this: "What advantage can I give to the Church and to the cause of the gospel *because* of who I am and what I have?"

The reference to *servant* in 2:7 is significant. Many years ago I conducted a Sunday school class on discipleship. Throughout the sessions I referred to disciples as slaves of Christ. After one class a man reproved me. "I am not a slave to Jesus," he protested. "I am not under compulsion. I freely give myself to Him. I am a servant, not a slave. To call me a slave is to demean my love for God and lower my loyalty to Him as mere conscripted service." His point was well taken.

Many translations (the NIV included) give the sense of "servant" when translating the Greek word *doulos*. Our service and love is to be voluntary. But we must not miss the connotation the Greek word *doulos* had in Jesus' and Paul's day.

At that time there were but three classes of people: the rich, the poor and the slaves. When we hear the word *servant,* we think of a paid staff person—perhaps a maid, a butler, a cook, a chauffeur. Servants of the first century would have had no such privileges. Society granted them no rights or privileges. A slave was fully dependent on and submissive to his or her owner. When Jesus relinquished His potential in glory for the incarnation, He took on Himself the attitude of a slave. And as such, Jesus put Himself in a position where He had no rights granted by society. His only right was the fulfillment of the Father's will. He had no privileges except the honor of being His Father's servant.

We are called to voluntarily add to our own potential the attitude of a slave. We are called to be people without rights save God's will, people without privileges save God's honor. We are to be fully at the disposal of others. We are to sacrifice our potential for the interests of others (cf. 2:3-4). The mind of Christ moves us beyond saying "I have a need" to saying, "I volunteer my services to meet your need."

Having the Mind of Christ Will Produce Useful Obedience

Is there a difference between plain obedience and *useful* obedience? I am making the distinction because being good is not enough. Following Christ is not just a call to believe and be good. Following Christ means believing and being good *for something.* Look again at the text: "Being found in appearance as a man, [Jesus] humbled himself and became obedient to death—even death on a cross!" (2:8).

As a Man, Jesus did not manifest merely a moral, good life. His life was also characterized by obedience. The great tragedy of the modern, "relevant," practical gospel of today, someone remarked, "is in calling many to belief but few to obedience."[6]

Is it any wonder that the Church is weak and that countless Christians wander aimlessly in search of meaning, self-esteem and self-potential? The gospel no longer calls people to repent, believe and obey. Now the appeal is, "Come to Christ and better yourselves," or "Come to Christ because God wants you to live up to your potential." Such exhortations fit our culture, but they are a far cry from what Paul urges in 2:6-8.

James D. Hunter, a University of Virginia sociologist, has written extensively on evangelicalism. He observes: "A total reversal has taken place in the evangelical conception of the nature and value of the self." Sixty-two percent of evangelical college students agree with the statement: "For the Christian, realizing your full potential as a human being is just as important as putting others before you." Sadly, this reflects a similar attitude among the evangelical community as a whole. More than half agree with the statement: "The purpose of life is enjoyment and personal fulfillment."[7]

I appreciate frankness. But I am alarmed by this perception of the Christian life. Can you imagine if Jesus had held to this attitude? All prospects of Bethlehem and Calvary would have ended in the mind of God. Jesus did not consider His own potential in glory as something to be weighed alongside a ministry to sinners, to those under God's judgment.[8]

Submit to Sacrificial Obedience

When Jesus added the attributes of a slave to His potential, He had a purpose in mind. Having the mind of Christ means that all we are—all our potential—is placed at God's disposal for the advantage of others.

Relatively few witnessed the 1995 bombing of the Federal Building in Oklahoma City. But most North Americans (and indeed people in other nations) lived the nightmare vicariously through the television pictures of rescue workers picking their way through the shattered building in search of victims. If those courageous rescuers had been considering their personal potential, they might not have risked their lives to save as many as possible.

It seems that today's evangelical pulpiteers and writers would have us conclude that sanctification leads to a place where the believer can be comfortable with himself or herself and fits nicely in our democracy. Rather, sanctification ought to lead us to the place where our potential can be sacrificed for the welfare of others. That is Paul's point. Jesus gave up His potential by placing Himself in a position of vulnerability, of service. Obedience to the point of death does not necessarily mean martyrdom. It is an obedience that exchanges any consideration of our personal potential for the welfare of others.

Aim at Redemptive Obedience
Paul adds a phrase to the original hymn: "even death on a cross!" Our obedience has aim, it has purpose. We have something to be obedient for, namely, the redemption of others. Not only does the Christ-life motivate us to live beyond our personal potential, the mind of Christ also provides direction for our obedience.

"Houston, We Have a Problem"
The words "Houston, we have a problem" bring back suspense-filled memories. I was only a kid, but I remember vividly the potentially tragic Apollo 13 mission. While three men were on their way to the moon, a series of events led to a near-fatal situation. Power was dwindling. Oxygen was in short supply. Their lives were being held in the balance.

Back in Houston Command Center, hundreds of men and women put their potentials on hold. They sacrificed sleep, personal time, energy. They harnessed talents and creativity. They forfeited natural rights and pleasures. All to bring three men back from the moon alive. They did it!

Our obedience to Christ is governed by God's redemptive purposes, the gospel. We have more than just three men whose lives are in the balance, who have lost their way. Are we making redemptive choices regarding our time, energy, creativity, potential? Are we harnessing what we have and who we are, adding the attribute of a servant for the redemptive purpose of God?

All of us face the dilemma of being stressed beyond the limit and stretched too thin. How do we determine when to say yes and when to say no to the countless time- and energy-consuming ventures of obedience and service? The answer lies in 2:8. Just because someone comes up with an idea as to how we can serve does not mean we are obligated to say yes. The text suggests that *we* see the needs and opportunities. We harness our potential and become obedient for the sake of others, especially for the sake of their redemption.

Is our relationship with Christ producing His attitude of humble service to others? Are we willing to sacrifice our potential—whether intellectual, athletic, business, political—in order to play a decisive, redemptive role in the lives of others? If so, we are progressing in our sanctification!

The Mind of Christ Means Pursuing God's Glory, Not Our Self-esteem

We confuse our culture's preoccupation with fulfillment with God's call to joyful obedience. The reasoning goes something like this: God wants me to be the best I can be *for Him.* I can't be my best unless I have a healthy self-image. I can't have a healthy self-image unless I build my self-esteem.

Most people link self-esteem to discovering and then realizing the fulfillment of their potential. I do not suggest we should ignore our insecurities and disappointments. When we develop basic *trust*—security—and have *real accomplishment,* we can change how we feel about ourselves. We can resist the demeaning things others say about us. We can withstand the false expectations placed on us.[9]

You ask, "Where can I find this trust?" "What is real accomplishment?" Our text provides the answers to those questions too:

> *Therefore God exalted him to the highest place*
> *and gave him the name*
> *that is above every name,*
> *that at the name of Jesus*
> *every knee should bow,*

> *in heaven and on earth*
> *and under the earth,*
> *and every tongue confess*
> *that Jesus Christ is Lord,*
> *to the glory of God the Father.* (2:9-11)

These verses inform us of Christ's exaltation and lordship over all things. None of us, of course, will experience this type of exaltation. What, then, do these verses mean? What purpose do they serve in Paul's exhortation to have the mind of Christ?

Allow for God's Vindication

This "exaltation" and the giving of a "name" speak of the resurrection of Jesus (cf. Ephesians 1:20-21; Acts 2:32-33; 5:30-31). We often turn to the resurrection as another proof of Jesus' deity. Although it is a proof of His deity, it serves a further apologetic purpose. It also proclaims to the world: "This Jesus, whom you thought to be a fool, a criminal, a traitor, a lunatic, whom you nailed to a cross, is really none of these. He is Messiah!" (see Acts 2:36). His appearance as a humble servant veiled His deity. But now everyone can see He is the King. The resurrection is God's way of saying, "Everybody was wrong, and Jesus was right!"

Although it looked foolish—or even unwise—at the time, Jesus' obedience to God's redemptive purpose was vindicated when He was resurrected. Likewise, in today's world, with all the expectations of self-fulfillment and success, setting aside one's potential can seem self-abasing, senseless, even ridiculous. That's because the Christian measure of a fulfilled life, a life lived to its full potential, is different from the standards and expectations set by our culture.

Jesus trusted God to exalt Him—to vindicate His obedience. We too can trust God to do the same. Peter reminds us:

*To this you were called, because Christ
suffered for you, leaving you an example,
that you should follow in his steps.*

*"He committed no sin, and no deceit
was found in his mouth." When they hurled
their insults at him, he did not retaliate; when
he suffered, he made no threats. Instead, he
entrusted himself to him who judges justly.*
(1 Peter 2:21-23)

Our energy, creativity, and time are not to be wasted
on pursuing what we suppose our potential is. God will
vindicate our lives lived in humble obedience to His
redemptive purposes. That is the trust that provides the
security we need for healthy self-respect.

Hunger for the Glory of God
The devil was the first to promote the idea of human potential. In the Garden of Eden, the serpent misled Adam and Eve
into wrongly reaching for their full potential. "God knows
that when you eat of [the forbidden fruit] your eyes will be
opened, and you will be like God, knowing good and evil"
(Genesis 3:5). Adam and Eve forgot that God's purpose for
them was to live for His glory—His pleasure (cf. Philippians
2:13, NASB)—not the fulfilling of their potential.

When we live for God's glory rather than for our
perceived potential, we will be more stable. We will be more
persevering. We will have more abundant joy. Jesus' death on
the cross did not hinder His potential. Just as Jesus hungered
for the glory of God, so must we. Therein is the "real accomplishment" we need in order to build healthy self-respect.

As my college graduation approached, I anticipated
a call to be the pastor of discipleship at a rather large
church. Already I had established an active discipleship
program and a singles' ministry. But I was passed over—for

a minister of music! I felt rejected, abused, confused and hurt. Afterward I enrolled in a good seminary where I thought my talents would shine. But I discovered that I was just one among a hundred shining students.

A Menial Job—Cleaning Toilets

Through my seminary years I worked part-time to help support my family. My job consisted of the two things I despise more than anything on earth: cleaning and vacuuming. I was a janitor. Already I was a wreck emotionally. The combination of being a nobody at school and a janitor for a daycare center made things worse. *I felt I was not fulfilling my potential.*

One day while cleaning a toilet I got angry at God. Slamming the sponge down into the toilet bowl, I said, "I am a preacher, a teacher. And here I am cleaning toilets!" I protested not getting the church position. I complained about not preaching. My insecurities matched my "unfulfilled potential." I knew I was dealing with pride, but I thought my complaint was justified because I did have gifts, you know!

In the midst of my tantrum, God brought to my mind a sermon illustration I had heard back at college. The preacher recalled the story of a rather well-to-do graduate student who finished top of his class with a doctorate. He felt called to the ministry, and a rather prestigious Philadelphia congregation invited him to be their pastor. But the young man felt called to work with William Booth in England. So he left America to apply for a ministry with the Salvation Army.

At the interview, Mr. Booth told the young man there was no place for him. His education and wealthy-status would hinder him from taking orders from street preachers, some of them former drunks and prostitutes. But the young man was persistent, and Mr. Booth gave him a try.

He sent him to a dark, dingy cellar to clean and shine the muddy boots of the street preachers.

After a while, it occurred to the young man that indeed he might be wasting his talents and gifts. "You call yourself a servant of God," the devil seemed to be saying, "but look at you. You're squandering all you have to offer." The man thought of the Philadelphia pulpit he had turned down. But as those thoughts danced in his head, another Voice whispered, "It's all right. I washed their feet too."

My Ego, Not My Potential, Was Offended

There at my daycare janitorial job, I realized the issue was pride and my false sense of fulfillment. It was my ego that had been offended, not my potential.

The United States and Canada have close to 300 million "most important persons in the whole world."[10] Logic would suggest someone's potential is going to be sacrificed. The mind of Christ turns this idea *right-side-up.* We must consider that the pursuit of our potential might actually be a disadvantage for others and a hindrance to the gospel. It is not self-fulfillment but self-submission that God desires.

But you say, "If I give myself to sacrificial obedience, I could be put in a position where I was taken advantage of. I could be used and, even worse, abused." That possibility exists. And it happens far too often. The solution is not to reject the biblical text and shrink from sacrificial service to others. The solution is to exercise the mind of Christ. Each of us has limited time, energy and resources. We should be selective. The Christ-hymn of Philippians 2 supplies the appropriate elements for the decision-making process.

- What's at stake? Realizing *my* full potential or the redemptive advantage of another?
- What's really being sacrificed? My rights? My

privileges? My potential? My pride?

- How will my decision further the cause of the gospel?
- Who else will be affected by my decision?
- How will my decision affect my church? Will it build up the congregation? Will it weaken the church?
- Which decision will bring most glory and honor to God?

Endnotes

[1] See Os Guinness, *The Dust of Death: A Critique of the Counter Culture* (Downers Grove, IL: InterVarsity, 1973), 22-23; also see Paul Johnson's chapter, "Relativistic Times," in *Modern Times: The World from the Twenties to the Eighties* (New York: Harper & Row, 1983), especially 47-48.

[2] Paul Vitz, "Leaving Psychology Behind," in *No God but God: Breaking with the Idols of Our Age,* Os Guinness and John Seel, eds. (Chicago, IL: Moody, 1993), 108.

[3] For example, see A.B. Simpson, "Wholly Sanctified," in *The Best of A.B. Simpson,* compiled by Keith M. Bailey (Camp Hill, PA: Christian Publications, 1987), 47-58. For a fuller discussion of the various views on sanctification, see Donald Alexander, *Christian Spirituality: Five Views of Sanctification* (Downers Grove, IL: InterVarsity, 1988).

[4] For a fuller discussion on the issues of Jesus' deity, preexistence and humanity contained in this text, see Gerald F. Hawthorne, *Word Biblical Commentary,* Vol. 43, *Philippians* (Waco, TX: Word, 1983) and Moises Silva, *Philippians* (Chicago, IL: Moody, 1988); see also Peter O'Brien, *The Epistle to the Philippians* (Grand Rapids, MI: Eerdmans, 1991) and Ralph Martin, *Philippians* (Greenwood, SC: The Attic Press, Inc., 1976).

[5] Hawthorne, 85. Hawthorne discusses why Jesus did not concede His position in glory but rather, because He was

God, poured Himself out on behalf of others.

6 Cited in *Beyond Cultural Wars: Is America a Mission Field or Battlefield?* (Chicago, IL: Moody, 1994), 64; see Hunter, *Evangelicalism: The Coming Generation* (Chicago: University of Chicago, 1987), 53; also the surveys in the appendix of David Wells, *God in the Wasteland: The Reality of Truth in a World of Fading Dreams* (Grand Rapids, MI: Eerdmans, 1994), 228-256.

7 Hunter, 53

8 Wells, 201.

9 Paul Vitz (see note 2), 97-98.

10 Ibid.

CHAPTER 7

Sanctification is a Community Event

Philippians 2:12-18

I N THE WORLD OF BASEBALL, the autumn of 1994 will live in infamy. Lamented Al Martin, a Pittsburgh Pirates player representative: "World War I couldn't stop the World Series. Neither could World War II. Even an earthquake couldn't stop it [referring to the destructive San Francisco quake in 1993]...It's almost too much to comprehend."

There were heated negotiations between player reps and owner reps (in posh, expensive hotels, of course!). And the greedy, selfish side of the North American character became all too evident.

Concessions on both sides finally resulted in an agreement. The players returned to the ballparks for the 1995 season.

But not the fans, as the sports commentators observed—at least, not in full measure. The fans felt let down, betrayed by the magnitude of greed among the players

and the organizational leadership. The baseball strike of
1994-95 revealed something about the North American character that seemed to make everyone a bit ashamed. Wars and
natural disasters couldn't stop baseball. But self-interest did.

I wonder if there is a lesson here for the Church.
North America is known for its multiple churches and
denominations. Hardly a crossroads is without its house of
worship. "Mega churches" boast of attendance in the thousands. Para-church ministries operate with multimillion-
dollar budgets. Why, then, in North America is the Christian
faith relegated to the irrelevant scrap heap of discarded
traditions, ideas, and values?[1] The Church can always
expect a measure of tension between the structures of the
world and itself. But its irrelevance is not persecution; it's
an indictment!

A Diminished Witness

Some are predicting that the real battle of this age will be
between Marxism, Islam and Third World Christianity.[2]
They consider the Western Church, especially in the United
States and Canada, too weak for any effective contribution
to the struggle for people's hearts and minds. The Church's
character has been weakened by its members' self-centered
pursuits and by the promotion of self-interests—personal,
denominational, and professional. Its witness is diminished
because its members are more concerned about their own
well-being than about the Church's.

Chuck Colson, in his book *The Body,* comments:

> When Christians in the early centuries gath-
> ered together, they became known as the
> *communio sanctorum,* meaning "the commu-
> nion of saints." And they were indeed that,
> bound together as only men and women
> could be who were surrounded by an angry,

hostile society ready to feed them to the lions. But by manifesting the church, they made visible the mystery of God's salvation, and this witness changed the world.[3]

Can the North American Church regain its effective witness, its relevance? Perhaps—if we who are its members recognize the vital relationship between the Church's health and the power of its witness.

Paul's letter to the Philippian church links the progress of the gospel to the vitality of the Church. And the apostle adds that the individual Christian's joyous perseverance cannot be separated from the Church's health. The Christ-hymn (2:6-11) that we looked at in chapter 6 is directly related to correcting the Church's indisposition (2:3). The action needed to return health to the Church (2:3-4) is to manifest the mind of Christ. This means that each Christian must imitate Jesus' humble, sacrificial, redemptive obedience (2:6-8).

As we proceed in Paul's letter, we will see that 2:12-18 relates our sanctification to the Church's health. This text continues our call to Christian citizenship (1:27ff.) and our mutual struggle for the faith of the gospel. As far as Paul is concerned, the heart of the issue is obedience. Christian obedience is necessary to restore the Church's vitality and its effective witness. Paul is exhorting the Church to renew its Christlike obedience—for the Church's health and the sake of the gospel.

Obedience for a Healthy Church

What questions occupy Christians' minds today? "How can I have an intimate relationship with God?" "Where can I find God's power for my life?" Questions such as these sound biblical and spiritual. In fact, they are vacuous. They actually betray our cultural preoccupation with the private sphere. Intimacy with God cannot be separated from the Christian's relationship to the Church. Nor does God grant "power" to fulfill self-interests. He grants power to fulfill His purposes.

Paul purposely joins his comments in 2:12-18 with the Christ-hymn (2:6-11) he has just quoted. Messiah Jesus displayed humility by becoming obedient to God's purposes (2:8). Now Paul acknowledges the Philippians' obedience (2:12). He addresses them, "My dear friends," and he refers to their past obedience ("as you have always obeyed"). Thus he causes them to reflect on their initial conversion (see Acts 16:14, 32-33).[4] Paul hopes his reference to their obedience will provoke the Philippians to renew their original commitment to Christ and the gospel.

The process of sanctification has been Paul's concern since 1:12, the progressive growth into the likeness of Christ. In 2:6-8 Paul sets forth the ways we should be imitating Christ Jesus. Now he reminds us that growing in the likeness of Christ implies an obedience that puts the church (one's local congregation in this case) above ourselves. A church may be torn apart or weakened by rivalry over status, conceit, arrogance, or self-interest. In such a case, the Holy Spirit seeks those who will stand together, show mutual care for each other, and serve each other for the sake of the gospel.

Philippians 2:12-18 reveals Paul's central concern—the health of the church. The church's health and well-being, our sanctification and the impact of the gospel are all interwoven. To ignore the church or in some way diminish the vitality of the church is in direct contradiction to the process of sanctification. Said another way, our sanctification will impact the members of our local church.

Our Sanctification Should Demonstrate Respect for Every Member of the Body

After steering the Philippian believers back to their original call—their first love—Paul says to them, "Work out your salvation with fear and trembling." Sometimes we need to hear the actual Greek word order. Say it aloud: *"With fear and trembling, your salvation, work it out."* Paul puts the verb last for emphasis. It is a serious matter our salvation to work out. We often simply respond to this text by adding, "Work out what God has worked in." We should note two things, however. One, this text is addressed to the whole congregation. The "you" is plural. That prompts the other points or questions: What is being worked in and how does the congregation work it out?

The phrase *"fear and trembling"* can have a wide range of connotations: fear of failure, nervous anxiety about one's responsibilities, awe and reverence in the presence of someone or something. Which best fits the context?

When fear and trembling are juxtaposed in this manner, they can suggest something positive rather than something negative. Only Paul, among New Testament writers, joins the two words. Nowhere does he use them to indicate an attitude we should have before God—that is, fearing and trembling before God. Invariably he uses them to indicate the disposition people should have toward each other (1 Corinthians 2:3; 2 Corinthians 7:15; Ephesians 6:5). Were we to give this idiomatic phrase a contemporary twist, it would be something like, "Have respect for each other."[5] In the broader context, Philippians 2:12 calls us to renew our obedience to Christ by showing mutual respect within our local church.

Present and Future Implications

Although some suggest that Paul means spiritual health by his reference to salvation, such a deviation from Paul's normal use of the word is not necessary.[6] *Salvation* refers to the full measure of God's dealing with humankind. Thus the word has both present and future implications. Although we are saved by faith now, our salvation and its full revelation will be realized on the day of the Lord, at the *eschaton*.[7] In other words, Paul is saying that salvation, if it is to be realized at the return of Christ, should characterize our lives now and the life of our churches now (1 Peter 1:7-9). Our relationship to God's salvation must not be divorced from our relationship to other Christians. We will demonstrate our personal salvation by how well we meet our obligations within our church community. Are we seeking the welfare of the body by manifesting mutual respect?

This interpretation fits the wider context of Philippians 1:12-2:4. Perseverance of the faith is a community project. Each Christian needs the support of other Christians. The individual is not being called to "work out" some form of salvation apart from the church. Since the final outcome at the last day shall reveal a glorious Church that will declare God's riches in Christ (Ephesians 2:7), we should work toward mutual respect among ourselves—now.

There is another parallel between the attitude of Christ (Philippians 2:6-8) and "working out [our] salvation." Remember how in 2:7 the word *himself* comes before the verb? The implication is that Jesus voluntarily poured Himself out. In 2:12 we have a similar idea. The word *your* in this verse has a corresponding grammatical priority in the Greek text. *Your* does not simply indicate whose salvation, but that each of us must freely, voluntarily choose to work toward mutual respect. In the same way sanctification is not some call to a vague concept of holiness or privatized obedience. It is a call to restore the health of the Church. Do not misunderstand me. Of course holiness and obedience are essential for growth in Christlikeness. The point, however, is that we often relegate such holiness and obedience to the private sphere. But the Bible always enjoins personal holiness and obedience in the context of public or community obligations. That is the biblical definition of being righteous!

Our Sanctification Should Display Integrity

We are inclined to relegate Christian integrity to moral and behavioral areas. Do not steal. Do not cheat. Do not lie. Keep yourself pure. Abstain from immoral behavior. These admonitions are certainly correct. But as long as Christian integrity is defined apart from the Church, such moralizing is vacuous. Christian integrity must be understood in terms of who we are corporately. How well do we relate as a church body to God's redemptive purposes? That is the real issue, not simply how well we behave individually.

Why be concerned about the Church's well-being? In 2:13-16 Paul reveals the depth and breadth of this vital relationship between the Church and our sanctification. He directs our attention, once more, to God's purpose, His will. "It is God who works in you to will and to act according to his good purpose" (2:13).[8] That verse explains why we are to work toward mutual respect within the church body—why we are to pursue harmony and each other's spiritual well-being. Why are we to do this? "Because God is the One who is working both to promote His goodwill (purpose) and to provide the ability to bring about such goodwill" (2:13, author's paraphrase).

This verse and 2:12 blend God's sovereign control and our human responsibility. There is no contradiction here, for divine action always seeks to provoke a human response. God's action should inspire our commitment both to support and to conform to such action.

God's Purpose: A Healthy Church

What is this "purpose" that God seeks to work out? The word is not normally translated "purpose" but rather "pleasure" or "goodwill."[9] Paul used the same word earlier (1:15) in describing the goodwill of those who supported his ministry. In a communication to Philippi, it is not possible to shake the connotation this word would have had in the minds of the recipients. Although Paul is speaking about God's purposes, His choice of this particular word would have indicated to the Philippians that God's purpose is the well-being—the health—of the church. Such certainly is the implication of 1:1-4 and 1:14-15.

Sense the flow of 2:12-13 read together:

Along with your salvation, achieve mutual respect within the church. Why? Because God is the One who is producing among all of you the potential and the work that produces His good pleasure—that is, the church's well-being. (Author's translation)

Most Christians at one time or another ask, "How can I find God's will for my life?" Most of the "methods" suggested to help us find God's will use a combination of Bible proof-texts, feelings (or notions) and signs (or situations). I find it amazing that we who are fallible, prone to selfishness and subject to sinful temptation (and, in our culture, inclined to comfort and self-esteem) rely so heavily on the subjective. It is even more surprising when we consider that God has graciously revealed His will through the Bible and the Living Word, Jesus Christ. We need never feel that God's will is somewhere far out there. Philippians 2:13 reveals once and for all until the end of time God's will for us. We are to join Him in achieving the Church's health, its well-being.[10]

Having confidence in God means we trust Him to bring about what He promised. Jesus Himself said, "I will build my church, and the gates of Hades will not overcome it" (Matthew 16:18). Despite the condition of the Church and the varied levels of health from church to church, God will work effectually to build His universal Church. He will bless and strengthen any endeavor or personal attitude that builds, renews, or enhances the vitality of His Church.

How do we show God's good pleasure? Next (Philippians 2:14-15) we have an imperative with a promise: "Do everything without complaining or arguing, so that you may become blameless and pure, children of God without fault..." Imperatives are to be obeyed. But they also are indicative of something. In this case, 2:14-15 describes God's people.

No More Complaining! No More Arguments!

In order to promote goodwill within the congregation and thus restore the church's health, the Christian community is to refrain from complaining (literally, grumbling) or arguing (literally, disputing). This reference to grumbling and disputing evokes images of the nation Israel as it journeyed through the Sinai desert. The people complained against Moses and doubted God's promises (Exodus 15-17; Numbers 14-17; 1 Corinthians 10:10). Whether Paul intends to make a direct parallel or not, one thing is certain. Such attitudes led the people to stray away from God and act immorally. Such attitudes caused Israel's enemies to blaspheme Yahweh God. Paul says "God was not pleased with most of them" (1 Corinthians 10:5).[11] If Israel's grumbling in the Sinai desert displeased God, the grumbling of the Philippians also was contrary to God's good pleasure. Such an attitude still is!

The broader Philippian context indicates that the church's poor condition (and the Christians' lack of joy) were the result of self-centeredness. Paul specifies the sins: complaining and disputing. As among the Israelites, this negative attitude was producing dissension, arrogance, and division (1 Corinthians 10:1-13). Thus it was harming the

body of believers. *Complaining* suggests dissatisfaction—
whispers (or protests) that promote ill will instead of goodwill (Acts 6:1; 1 Peter 4:9). *Disputing* suggests divisive
words prompted by evil thoughts and dark intentions, manifested in contentious arguments.[12] We fulfill the Philippians
2:14 command by bringing about the things that will gener-
ate goodwill among God's people. This pleases God. In any
activity of their shared fellowship Christians must not
engender attitudes of contention or futile disputes. Rather,
they are to be "children of God."

Paul's reference in 2:15 to "children of God"
implies a family resemblance. We bear God's likeness. That
is why we are to be above blame, pure and without fault.
Not that we will be free from false accusations or even from
deserved blame. But certainly we are not to bring such accusations on ourselves because of sinful, unrighteous, or
worldly behavior (1 Peter 2:11-17; 2 Corinthians 6:1-10).
The testimony of God resides in the Church. We bear God's
image. Our "love for one another" and our participation in
the gospel (that is, our love for those outside the Church) is
a communication loud and clear.

Where is the Church to be the Church? Jesus said to
His Father, "My prayer is not that you take them out of the
world but that you protect them from the evil one. They are
not of the world, even as I am not of it" (John 17:15-16). In
a similar way Paul exhorts the Philippian church. On the
one hand, they are not to be "complaining or arguing" (that
is, not of the world). On the other hand, they are to be the
Church, above reproach, amid "a crooked and depraved
generation" (that is, in the world).

More Old Testament Examples
Paul continues to draw upon images from Israel's exodus
from Egypt. The reference to "a crooked and depraved
generation" is an allusion to Deuteronomy 32:5:

*They have acted corruptly toward him; to
their shame they are no longer his children,
but a warped and crooked generation.*

Moses was saying that those Israelites who rebelled against God and were unrepentant of their "grumbling" were in fact not God's people at all. In quoting Moses, Paul certainly had in mind the false apostles who were belittling his ministry and causing havoc within the Philippian congregation (Philippians 1:15-17). Those were not God's people. Yet despite their contentiousness, the true congregation (3:3) must be faithful followers of Christ Jesus. They are God's people, who "look…to the interests of others" (2:4) and demonstrate Christlike obedience (2:8). Paul most assuredly also had the pagan, Gentile world in view. The Church must remain the Church in the midst of a perverse society that has refused or twisted the truth of God (Acts 13:10; 20:30).

The Church is God's light bearer in a perverse world and among false teachers. God's people are to "shine like stars in the universe" (Philippians 2:15). Here Paul turns to positive imagery. "Shining stars" suggest the torches that lit the dark nights or harbor beacons that warned of dangerous rocks. Paul is exhorting the Philippians to shine the gospel in the darkness of the world. In the world God's truth is absent. In the Church God's truth is manifest. We are to expose the dark world to the light of God's truth by being the Church. This is our witness.

But how can the Church witness to God's truth if it is more concerned about its pride, its self-interests and its status? Restoring the Church—bringing health to the Church—means restoring its witness. So the Church that is the light is to display its sacrificial and redemptive obedience, its good works of harmony, selflessness and humble service to others. Then it will be an influence for good in a corrupt and darkened world (Matthew 5:14; Ephesians 5:8;

1 Thessalonians 5:5).[13]

There should be no doubt that Paul is also warning the congregation. The author to the Hebrews asks: "How shall we escape if we ignore such a great salvation?" (Hebrews 2:3). Paul's language in Philippians reminds us of the dangers of disobedience. We are to remember that the Church and the gospel are at stake. When we do not seek the Church's health, we cannot expect that we will display God's truth in a darkened, perverse world. Consequently, we compromise our very purpose in the world.

How Does the Church Sustain Its Health?

How does the Church sustain its health? The Church sustains its health and maintains its witness as its members "hold out the word of life" (Philippians 2:16). The "word of life" has the emphatic position. We cling to, we grasp with all our might the word that gives us life. Paul is referring, of course, to that very instrument by which the Church receives the life of God, namely, the gospel. Word (*logos*) is often used as a direct equivalent for "gospel."[14]

The gospel, God's word, must have a central place—*the* central place—in the life of the Church. Walter Kaiser, an Old Testament scholar and preacher, points to the cause of our weakness (and, I would add, our lack of relevance):

> It is no secret that Christ's church is not at all in good health in many places of the world. She has been languishing because she has been fed, as the current line has it, "junk food."…As a result, theological and biblical malnutrition has affected [us]…[A] world-wide spiritual famine resulting from the absence of any genuine [diet] of the Word of God continues to run wild and almost unabated in most quarters of the church.[15]

David Wells, a professor at Gordon-Conwell Theological Seminary, sadly observes: "I have watched [over the years] as the evangelical church has cheerfully plunged into astounding theological illiteracy."[16] The sustaining power and life of the Church nowadays rests not in the gospel or the Word of God, but in worldly structures of prosperity, the popular therapeutic culture and the North American gods of earthbound bureaucracies, happiness and personal freedom.

Throughout Church history God has brought about reformation. He has strengthened the Church when Christians abandoned self-centeredness and held to the centrality of the Word. We cannot expect biblical Church growth, joyous spirituality or a healthy Church unless, like Martin Luther, the great reformer, we say with conviction, "My conscience is captive to the Word of God." We must rediscover our dependency on God's truth if we are to see the world affected by our light. As Jacques Ellul reminds us, "Anyone wishing to save humanity must first of all save the Word."

Our Sanctification Should Include a Shared Sacrifice

Paul ends this exhortation with a personal testimony concerning his relationship to the Philippian church. He desires their restoration, he says, "...that I may boast on the day of Christ that I did not run or labor for nothing" (2:16). His personal testimony is a model for fulfilling all that he has been speaking of in 2:1-16. It will return health to the Church and joy to the Christian life—a shared sacrifice:

> *But even if I am being poured out like a drink offering on the sacrifice and service coming from your faith, I am glad and rejoice with all of you. So you too should be glad and rejoice with me.* (2:17-18)

Paul is "glad" he can be a "poured out...drink offering." But his testimony is instruction and exhortation as well, for he asks the Philippians to "be glad and rejoice" with him.

Elsewhere Paul speaks of Christian service or church ministry as an "offering" (see Romans 12:1; 15:16). The apostle even refers to the Philippians' gift as an act of sacrificial service (Philippians 4:10, 18; 2 Corinthians 8:2). His reference to being "poured out like a drink offering" indicates he saw himself as participating in God's redemptive purpose. Paul's ministry to the Philippians enabled them to provide sacrifices and service that flowed from their own faith. Paul delights—rejoices—in his glad obedience to the gospel, even if it means being poured out as a drink offering. The reason? When his sacrifice is added to the Philippians' sacrifice, the sum works to widen the gospel's influence.

A survey asked American baby boomers, "What do you want out of life?" The most common answer came back, "More!" The problem, however, is that this same group, while desiring "more," wants to do less and be commitment-free. Church growth specialists now encourage the Church, if they want to "attract" these new consumers of religion, to neither expect nor demand "commitment" from them. This, however, is contrary to the biblical image of the Church. It is demonstrative of our continued compromise with the world.

Commitment is what Christianity is all about. Christian faith and commitment to Christ are not just private, inner matters of the soul. Paul's instruction here indicates that faith and commitment are outward, public pledges to the Church body. The Christian life must by definition include service and obligation (Romans 1:14-17).

The Gospel's Greatest Ally

In the *Screwtape Letters,* C.S. Lewis reveals a fictional communication between a superior demon, Screwtape, and one of his underling field workers, Wormwood. In one exchange of correspondence, Screwtape compares the weak church and the strong Church:

> One of the great allies at present is the church itself. Do not misunderstand me. I do not mean the Church as we see her spread out through all time and space and roots in eternity, terrible as an army with banners. That, I confess, is a spectacle that makes our boldest tempters uneasy. But fortunately it is quite invisible to these humans.[17]

Lewis understands that *the* Church is the underworld's fierce enemy. But the church-turned-inward is the underworld's greatest ally. Unfortunately, the average American Christian is unaware of this insight. He or she is too preoccupied with self-interests and pursuing the North American dream.

Robert Coles, a Harvard psychologist and a committed Christian, writes: "Adjustment and adaptation is so often an acquiescence to the most banal and crude, if not blasphemous, in a given society."[18] That is why Chuck Colson points out that "the feel-good, restore-your-self-worth, therapeutic gospel is so dangerous." This modern gospel turns the Church inward, causing the individual Christian to weigh all cost and commitment against his or her well-being.[19] More often than not, the Church is shortchanged.

In Philippians 2:12-18, Paul links Christian sanctification to the life of the Church. We, however, have allowed ourselves to be bought off with democratic freedom, material prosperity, tax deductions and constitutionally guaranteed rights and freedoms.[20] Many are concerned about the Church in its present state and its need for a Spirit-awakening. In our narcissistic age we would do well to reevaluate our level of commitment to Christ and His Church. The truly sanctified will seek the well-being of the Church, their own local fellowship particularly.

A High Priority

The renewing of the congregation where we worship should be a high priority. Our own intimacy with God depends on it. The Church's relevance and witness depends on it. Howard Snyder once observed:

> Many churches do not share the gospel effectively because their communal experience is too weak and tasteless to be worth sharing...But where *Christian fellowship demonstrates the gospel,* believers become alive and sinners get curious and want to know what the secret is.[21]

A serious, deeper Christian life must be concerned about the Church. The restoration of the Church—especially our local church—is part of God's sanctifying work in us. Remember, sanctification is a community project. And the development of God's community—the local church—is essential to spiritual growth.

The building of a Christian community is revolutionary. It demands commitment. Jim Wallis reminds us that building any community is

> ...revolutionary because it proposes to detach men and women from their dependence upon the dominant institutions, powers and idolatries of the world system

over the lives of people.[22]

That comment lines up with Paul's juxtaposition of sanctification and Church life. For the process of sanctification is in part the relinquishing of our dependence on the expectations, structures and democratic guarantees in exchange for the life of the gospel. And the Church is the place where the life of the gospel is shared and propagated.

Philippians 2:12-18 is a clear text regarding the Christian's obligation to have a mind for the Church. For the sake of the Church, let us voluntarily relinquish our baby boomer expectations and our political rights. Let us allow God to renew our churches—the fellowships we attend—through personal repentance and a fresh partaking of the Christ-life. Let us think more highly of God's community. Let us share in the sacrifice that rejuvenates the Church's strength and awakens the world.

Endnotes

[1] There is evidence that despite the church growth movement and the presence of many megachurches, actual church attendance has not risen significantly above the 1937 average. See David Wells, *God in the Wasteland: The Reality of Truth in a World of Fading Dreams* (Grand Rapids, MI: Eerdmans, 1994), 78-79.

[2] This has changed somewhat since the fall of the Berlin Wall. Marxism, however, is still a fierce competitor in the arena of truth, especially in its more American form of simple social-atheism. I would add as well to this list the powerful force of New Age thinking. See David Watson, *Called and Committed: World-Changing Discipleship* (Wheaton, IL: Harold Shaw, 1982), 1. For a good critique of the Church's relevance and American attitudes, see Os Guinness' two books, *The American Hour: A Time of Reckoning and the Once and Future Role of Faith* (New

York: The Free Press, 1993), especially chapters 8-14 and 19-21, and *Fit Bodies, Fat Minds: Why Evangelicals Don't Think and What to Do about It* (Grand Rapids, MI: Baker, 1994).

[3] Charles Colson, *The Body: Being Light in Darkness* (Dallas, TX: Word, 1992), 69.

[4] Gerald F. Hawthorne, *Word Biblical Commentary,* Vol. 43, *Philippians* (Waco, TX: Word, 1983), 98.

[5] Ibid., 99-100.

[6] For opposing discussions on this idea, see Hawthorne, 100, and Moises Silva, *Philippians* (Chicago, IL: Moody, 1988), 138.

[7] Already saved, Ephesians 2:5, 8; Titus 3:5; will be saved, Romans 5:9-10; 1 Corinthians 3:15; 5:5; 2 Timothy 4:18; 1 Peter 1:9.

[8] The words *in you* should be understood to mean "among you [i.e., the Philippian congregation]." The *you* is plural and should be understood corporately rather than personally: "It is God who works in you to will and to act according to his good purpose" (2:13).

[9] A syntactical-linguistic study of the phrase *huper tes eudokúas* (2:13) indicates that Paul intended a semantic relationship between God's purpose and the Church's well-being. It is variously translated "for His good pleasure" (NASB, KJV), "according to His good purpose" (NIV), "to obey his good pleasure" (Good News). In Romans 10:1, Paul uses the word to indicate his "desire" to reach the Jews. In Second Thessalonians 1:11, it points toward the fulfilling of "all [their] pleasure" or "good purposes." In Ephesians 1:5, it is a synonym for God's will. In the Philippians passage, there is no doubt that God's "purpose" is meant, but Paul uses the term to develop as well the connotation of the Church's "goodwill." Hawthorne translates 2:13, "For the one who effectively works among you creating both the desire and drive to promote goodwill is God" (101). The

preposition *huper* never means "according to" (NIV) or "for" (NASB). Where the only subject is a prepositional phrase, as in 2:13, it is used to indicate that which a person (in this case, God) wants to attain. The context is clear. The exhortation is a call to harmony, unity, and goodwill toward others. See Ralph P. Martin's comment on this text in *New Century Bible Commentary, Philippians* (Grand Rapids, MI: Eerdmans, 1980). Martin correctly translates 2:13, "[It is God who] produces the will to amend the condition of His people and brings about the accomplishment of this state of 'goodwill'."

[10] Throughout the New Testament this same thought is understood as building the Church, increasing the Church or the gospel, serving the saints, etc.

[11] The verb form of *eudokúas* ("pleasure," "purpose") in 2:13 is used in First Corinthians 10:5, making the contexts similar.

[12] Hawthorne, 101.

[13] Ibid., 103.

[14] The "word" is synonymous with the gospel (Philippians 1:14; Acts 4:31; 6:2, 7; 8:14; 11:1, 12:24; 13:5, 7, 44, 46; 17:13; 18:11; 19:20; Ephesians 1:13; Colossians 1:5, 25; 3:16; 1 Timothy 1:6).

[15] Walter Kaiser, *Toward an Exegetical Theology* (Grand Rapids, MI: Baker, 1981), 7-8.

[16] David Wells, *No Place for Truth* (Grand Rapids: Eerdmans, MI,1993), 12. For a description of the modern evangelical American church's dependency on "worldly" cultural structures and attitudes, see David Wells, *God in the Wasteland: The Reality of Truth in a World of Fading Dreams* (Grand Rapids, MI: Eerdmans, 1994), 37-59.

[17] C.S. Lewis, *The Screwtape Letters* (Westwood, NJ: Barbour, 1961).

[18] Quoted by Charles Colson, 46.

[19] Ibid., 46-47.

[20] For a comprehensive study on both the American Christian's and the American pagan's modern idolatry, see Herbert Schlossberg, *Idols for Destruction: Christian Faith and Its Confrontation with American Society* (Nashville, TN: Thomas Nelson, 1983). See also Os Guinness and John Seel, *No God but God: Breaking with the Idols of Our Age* (Chicago: Moody Press, 1993).

[21] My emphasis. Howard Snyder, *The Community of the King* (Downers Grove, IL: InterVarsity, 1977), 125.

[22] Jim Wallis, *Agenda for Biblical People* (New York: Harper and Row, 1976), 103.

CHAPTER 8

Resolving to Live with All My Might
Philippians 2:19-30

B IOGRAPHIES, AUTOBIOGRAPHIES AND THE diaries of great Christian men and women fascinate me. Giants such as John Wesley, George Whitefield, David Brainerd and Jonathan Edwards captivate me. I am convicted, motivated and humbled by the accounts of those whom God has greatly used to promote His cause and increase His kingdom. In eternity I am sure we will learn of countless others unmentioned in the history books and unnoticed by the general public.

Jonathan Edwards, born in 1703, enrolled at Yale at age thirteen. He was a key instrument through whom God brought a great spiritual awakening to colonies that had become careless about the faith of their forefathers. His influence was felt in much of New England, New York and New Jersey. Eventually Edwards was asked to become president of Princeton College, a school then devoted to training church leaders. The life of this incredible man of God ended one month after he arrived at his new post. Ah, but what a life!

Jonathan Edwards has been the subject of many biographies. All seek to discover what motivated him, what drove him, what fed his passion. For answers, we must return to Yale College and note the aspirations of this young student. Edwards was convinced he must make some resolutions in the presence of his God. The list numbered seventy items, all of which he committed to memory.

Resolution 6 summarizes the passion of Edwards' heart: "Resolved to live with all my might while I yet live."[1]

In pondering that resolution we must keep two things in context. First, life to young Edwards was a gracious gift from God. Second, all of his resolves were made in the consciousness that God was looking on. His first resolution, in fact, was to "do whatsoever I think to be most to the glory of God." Since God's honor and glory were at stake in his life, Edwards further resolved "to find out fit objects of liberty and charity." Further, he would "live so as I shall wish I had done when I come to die."

Resolve Is a Mark of Discipleship

Our do-your-own-thing culture does not promote resolves like those, not even among the Christian population. A society and a church that measure life in terms of acquired happiness cannot grasp the depth of Edwards' conviction, nor his resolve.

An ad for a recent movie stated: "Everybody dies. Not everybody really lives." Edwards understood that long before Hollywood's money-seeking moguls came along. History, every once in a while, is graced by those who resolve to live with all their might—*for God.*

The New Testament is replete with such followers of Jesus Christ. The letter to the Philippians actually is structured around such models of resolve. The Philippians were overwhelmed by self-concern. They had neglected the "welfare of others." Paul addressed this attitude through the testimony of those who resolved to serve the Church. Without question the apostle Paul models such a life. We can hear his resolve in his concern for the Philippian congregation (1:3-11, 27-30) and for the gospel (1:12-26). The Christ-hymn focuses on the Premier Servant (2:6-11). And now the apostle illustrates how the Church and the gospel have benefited from two models of resolve: Timothy and Epaphroditus (2:19-30).

Philippians is very much a missionary newsletter written by Paul, the church planter, to a congregation who has faithfully supported his endeavors. He nevertheless harnesses his "missionary stories" to illustrate the major concerns that he addresses throughout the letter.

In 2:19-30, Paul commends Timothy and Epaphroditus, two proven coworkers. Paul regards them as servants of Jesus Christ and models of faith, industry, and *resolve*. He knows that if the strife-weary and anxious Philippian Christians will only emulate the discipleship characteristics of these two men, they will have no time for pride or anxiety. Through their joyous participation in the task of the gospel the Church will soon be returned to health.

Resolve: To Live with All Our Might
We do not lack for sermons and books on the topic of discipleship. Some Christians speak about discipleship as if it is something to be *into*—like being into politics or running or weight loss. But such a view of discipleship betrays some faulty assumptions.

First, we tend to formulate the call to discipleship as an option for Christians to consider. And second, there is a tendency (especially in today's consumer-oriented churches) to make discipleship attractive. The fact is, there is nothing attractive about discipleship. It calls for an undivided loyalty to the gospel. It calls people to place themselves at the disposal of the Church and its work. Dietrich Bonhoeffer said it best: "When Christ calls a man, he bids him come and die."

Both Timothy and Epaphroditus exemplify what J.B. Phillips remarked about the early Church:

> Perhaps because of their very simplicity, perhaps because of the readiness to believe, to obey, to give, to suffer and if need be to die, the Spirit of God found what He must always be seeking—a fellowship of men and women so united in faith and love that He can work in them and through them with the minimum of...hindrance.[2]

What Paul implies in his descriptions of these two men indicates what the true Christian life is. The deeper Christian life is a call to discipleship, a call to authentic Christian living. Whereas sanctification is the process (and progress) of becoming more like Christ, discipleship is the *discipline,* the lifestyle of the one who is becoming more like Christ. As we make our way through 2:19-30, we will discover the marks of the true disciple of Jesus Christ.

Paul certainly is informing his friends back in Philippi about his situation. But in doing so he uses special words to describe Timothy and Epaphroditus. He wants the Philippians to know these two men are models of the Christ-hymn Paul earlier cited (2:6-11). The narrative implies instruction. We should resolve to give the Church and the gospel priority (2:1-4, 12-18).

Resolve: To Put the Interests of Christ First
Paul and Timothy had a very special relationship.[3] It is indicated in the letter's salutation, where Paul accords partner status to Timothy (1:1). Evidently Timothy was with Paul in Rome. Since the apostle was under house arrest rather than

in prison, he was free to receive visitors (Acts 28:30-31). Timothy was Paul's young protégé. Although Paul found friendship and comfort in Timothy's presence, he was determined to send him back to Philippi.[4] Timothy would be Paul's spokesperson regarding the matters affecting the congregation. And later Timothy would report back to Paul (2:19).

But Timothy was more than simply an apostolic emissary. He demonstrated as well the "mind" or attitude that Paul wanted the Philippian congregation to emulate. Paul remarks, "I have no one else like him, who takes a genuine interest in your welfare. For everyone looks out for his own interests, not those of Jesus Christ" (2:20-21).

No doubt Paul was drawing upon his previous exhortation concerning "the interests of others" (2:4) and, as well, the implications of the Christ-hymn (2:6-7). When Paul looked at the pool of human resources available to him there in Rome, he found it very limited. He had "no one else of kindred spirit" (NASB). Both the NIV and NASB translators struggle to render a very complicated set of words. *Isopsychon,* the word translated "kindred spirit" (NASB) and "like him" (NIV), is a compound word meaning literally "of equal soul." In other words, Paul was describing Timothy as a soul mate, one who shared the same feeling or mind-set concerning the Church.[5]

Throughout 1:3-2:18, Paul has indicated the "mind" we are to have in order to give strength to the Church and increase the gospel.[6] Now he tells the Philippians that Timothy is the only one who has "a genuine interest in [their] welfare" (2:20). Timothy's *interest* is the Church's *welfare*; the health of the Church is uppermost in his mind. He shares Paul's own desire in this respect. His "genuine interest" coincides with Paul's earlier exhortation to the Philippians to "look . . . to the interests of others" (2:4).

In 1:27, Paul says the Philippian church's faithfulness

to Christ Jesus is gauged by their unity in "contending as one man" (*mia psyche*) for Christ's gospel. In 2:2, Paul confronts their self-centeredness by encouraging them as a congregation to be "like-minded" (*sumpsychoi*), literally, "co-souled" in purpose.

Insight into the Heart of Jesus

Clearly 2:20-21 gives us insight into the heart of Jesus Christ. Anyone concerned about His interests dares not ignore these two verses. It is clear that the person who confesses a genuine desire to live for Christ must have a genuine interest in His Church. Paul's own high regard for the Church is indisputable. Nor can we escape the fact that our joy and perseverance are bound together with the health and welfare of the Body of Christ, the Church.

The latter part of 2:20 is very difficult to translate. Wooden-literally it reads: "who will genuinely show concern (or care or anxiety) over the things concerning you." Paul chooses a word to describe Timothy's concern for the Church that is rarely used in a positive way. The word *interest*—"takes a genuine interest in your welfare"—means "to show worry" or "to show anxiety" (*merimnesei*).[7] It is used to indicate the weight of pressure or anxiety that flows out of Timothy's deep, genuine love for the church in Philippi. Elsewhere Paul uses the same word to indicate his own overwhelming sense of burden for the well-being of all the churches: "Besides everything else, I face daily the pressure of my concern [*merimna*] for all the churches" (2 Corinthians 11:28).

Often Christians will say, "I love the Church." Yet what they mean by *Church* is the nebulous, mystical Body of Christ, the Church universal. Their declaration sounds pious and, at first, spiritual. But it may simply mask their non-commitment to *a* church, to a local body of Christ. We can casually confess to love *the* Church and then refrain from loving *a* church.

We can also profess to love our local church but refrain from loving certain members of it. Frequently we are reminded that we need to love people. It is easy enough to love humankind as an idea or as a concept. Loving specific people or a specific person may be more difficult.[8]

Some of our secular friends can leave a spouse unloved, children neglected, immediate neighbors uncared for while they crusade altruistically for human rights. But are we less inconsistent if we violate our same responsibilities to do "church work"? Paul's words in Philippians 2:19-21 cry out for contextual interpretation and application. Simply put, anyone who is not concerned about a *local* church—and all its members—is not concerned about the interests of Jesus Christ.

Resolve: To Learn Submission and Servanthood

When I became a Christian in 1978, I was rather naïve. I knew my salvation depended solely on the work of Jesus Christ. The Bible was clear enough on that point. But I also supposed the same Bible that instructed me how to be saved would instruct me how to live "saved." It does and it doesn't. (I'll explain that in a moment.) That is where I was naïve.

As a newborn Christian, I was immediately placed under the spiritual care of the two men who led me to the Lord: Mike Cronk and Jack Anderson. In my naïveté, I assumed this was how all new Christians were taught. Such a submissive, teacher-pupil relationship with those more experienced and mature in the faith was standard procedure. It struck me as both biblical and reasonable. If growing in the faith is the process of learning submission to Christ's authority, then the issue of my autonomy must be resolved by learning such submission.

Later I discovered that new Christians rarely were put in such a discipleship environment. Yet both Jesus in the

Gospels and the apostles who wrote the New Testament letters clearly advocate such a relationship. I, a new Christian, was to be accountable to another, more mature Christian. Why, then, wasn't the church providing disciplers for its new converts?

Many years later, as a Bible college professor, I constantly heard students decrying the lack of discipleship between professors and students. I could agree with the students that little resembling true discipleship was going on in that academic setting. But I also realized the students were using the term *discipleship* outside its biblical implications. They more or less understood the term as a relationship with someone who'd teach them about the Bible. He or she would pray with them, encourage them to pray, help them memorize Bible verses and offer Christian advice.

During a student retreat this subject (and complaint) was discussed at length. Finally I asked the students, "When you say you want to be discipled, do you realize that such a teacher-disciple relationship means that you are to submit to the authority of the one discipling you?"

The room suddenly fell silent. But the students had gained a more biblical perspective of what is involved in discipleship.

Jesus' mandate, "Go and make disciples of all nations" (Matthew 28:19), can be seen in relationships throughout the New Testament. The first is Jesus and His disciples, of course. But there was also Barnabas, the discipler of Paul. And Paul, in turn, who discipled Timothy. Paul, founder of the Philippian church, has already indicated Timothy's selflessness. Timothy was one of the few who put the interests of the Church above all else. He did so because he was concerned about the interests of Jesus Christ. Now we are told the secret behind so selfless an attitude. Paul's partner in the service of the gospel learned this attitude through his relationship to Paul: "You know that

Timothy has proved himself, because as a son with his father he has served with me in the work of the gospel" (Philippians 2:22).

Timothy: A Proven Servant

Timothy had "proved himself" as a worthy servant of the Lord. Paul's decision to send Timothy to Philippi is based on his past record of service. Paul could count on Timothy. He could entrust Timothy with the welfare of the Church. The word *proved* (*dokime*) is used exclusively by Paul. It indicates both the process of testing and the result of such testing. In Second Corinthians Paul refers to the "tested character" of the Macedonian churches (Philippi was a Macedonian church!). "Out of the most severe trial," he said, "their overflowing joy and their extreme poverty welled up in rich generosity" (2 Corinthians 8:2). And Paul tells the Roman Christians that testing produces proven, persevering character: "We know that suffering produces perseverance; perseverance, character; and character, hope" (Romans 5:3-4).[9]

Paul holds up Timothy as one whom the Philippian church should emulate. He does so after his call for unity within the corporate body. Implied in his statement is the remedy for disunity: a father-son relationship. There are two implications here for Christian discipleship as well as for returning unity and joyous participation in the gospel to the Church.

First, the father-son relationship implies that Timothy had learned to serve. Literally, Paul says that Timothy "worked like a slave with me" (Philippians 2:22, author's translation). Earlier, Paul referred to Jesus as the premier Servant-Slave.[10] Now he points out that such imitation of Christ, such servanthood, is learned in a relationship with another who has already learned servant-hood. And it was in this relationship that Timothy had proved himself.

Second, the father-son relationship was not just a quaint metaphor. In Paul's day the term would have elicited the common image of a son learning his father's trade. Most likely Paul intended his readers to understand that Timothy learned not only how to serve but how to participate in the gospel. That, after all, was Paul's "trade" (1:5).

It is neither an accident nor incidental that Paul includes these "ministry" illustrations midstream in his letter. The context has been, thus far, an appeal for unity and recommitment to the task of the Church. Therefore the Timothy illustration suggests that such relationships, multiplied throughout the congregation, would get the church back on track. Likewise today, Christians need to be in "father-son" relationships where leaders lead others in demonstrations of *servanthood*. This would keep the Church leadership humble. It would teach the younger Christians how to participate in the work of the Church—with joy. Such discipleship relationships would curtail self-interest and self-autonomy throughout the congregation.

Resolve: To Risk Loss for Christ's Cause

We dare not view Paul's reference to Epaphroditus as merely the acknowledgement of a fine Christian worker. Paul intended more. His description of Epaphroditus indicates the character of one who fulfills the Christ-hymn. The way in which Paul fashions this missionary story suggests as much. He will soon be telling the Philippians that Epaphroditus risked his life for the sake of the mission:

- *"Indeed he was ill, and almost died"* (2:27)
- *"He almost died for the work of Christ"* (2:30)
- *"risking his life"* (2:30)

During the bloodshed in Bosnia, a U.S. fighter jet, piloted by a young American, was downed by missile fire.

There were rumors that another pilot who saw the explosion thought he saw an open parachute through the thick clouds. But he was not sure. There was no reported word from the missing pilot. His family and friends prayed for a miracle.

Meanwhile, the American military was alerted to a faint radio call—perhaps from the downed pilot. The navy sent in one of its crack rescue teams, and the miracle happened. Captain Scott O'Grady was recovered and restored to family and friends. What a story it was!

Why would a group of able-bodied men risk their lives to rescue *one* person? Let's create an imaginary interview with the captain of the rescue team:

> "Sir, why risk your life and the lives of your men for this one pilot? Isn't that foolish?"
>
> *"It was not a question of our lives, but a question of our mission. It is the mission that counts. We resolve that our lives will be at risk for the mission."*

We cheered the rescue with scarcely a thought that those on the rescue team could have exchanged their lives for the pilot's—or, worse, in a futile attempt to save the pilot.

Epaphroditus understood such risks. He put his life on the line for one man—Paul.

A Gospel Participant

Epaphroditus most likely hand-carried the letter Paul was writing to the Philippians. We are not told whether he knew its contents. But the Philippians would have in the person of Epaphroditus an example of what it takes to "participate in the gospel" and thus return persevering joy to the congregation. His grave illness was directly related to fulfilling "the work of Christ" (2:30).

Paul uses some very pertinent words to describe Epaphroditus. He calls him "my brother, fellow worker and fellow soldier, who is also your messenger, whom you sent to take care of my needs" (2:25).[11] We do not wish to burden such language with deeper meaning than it carries. But in the context of this particular letter, such acknowledgments are a corrective to the Philippians' thinking.

In referring to Epaphroditus as a *fellow worker,* Paul indicates that he is someone with whom he shares the ministry of the gospel. *Fellow soldier* suggests someone who is fighting side by side with the apostle. Consequently Epaphroditus shares in the consequences of the "fight" (1:28-30; Romans 16:3, 7; 2 Timothy 2:3; Philemon 2).

The New International Version translates the *apostolos,* the phrase describing Epaphroditus, as "messenger." The New Testament writers, especially Paul, apply this word very narrowly. Normally it designates those called to the special position of apostle.[12] Attempts to broaden the scope of the word (as the NIV translators have done) mask the impact Paul might have been attempting to make. Certainly Epaphroditus was not a church-planting, foundation-laying apostle. But the reference here might well have indicated that "relationships within the Church must not be measured in terms of superiority or inferiority, but of equality."[13] Just as Timothy shared in sending the letter (Philippians 1:1), so Epaphroditus shares equally in the apostolic task by providing Paul with life-sustaining food.

From Messenger to Minister

The Philippians had sent Epaphroditus to Paul with money for food and clothing. Prisoners of the Roman Empire did not enjoy the tax-payer-funded care that those in North American prisons take for granted. If relatives or friends did not supply clothing and food, the prisoner went without. In his letter to the Philippians Paul refers to Epaphroditus as their "minister" to his needs. Paul uses the word *leitourgos*. It refers to a public servant who holds office at his own expense. He seems to be pointing out Epaphroditus' selfless service. The word draws as well on Old Testament imagery of the priesthood and the system of sacrifices.[14] In 4:18, Paul calls the gift Epaphroditus brought to him a "sacrifice." Thus Epaphroditus was performing a priestly function by supplying Paul's needs while he was incarcerated.

This heightened reference to a simple care package indicates that participation in the gospel does not necessarily mean activity dubbed great, awesome or inspiring. Just providing practical care to those directly involved in the advance of the gospel (again 1:5) qualifies. A statement like this would have spoken loudly to those who claimed certain superior spiritual gifts or positions. If Christians would emulate Epaphroditus and his service, super-Christian mentality would be crucified, and pride and status would be rendered ineffective.

These descriptions of Epaphroditus strongly suggest an equality of ministry, no matter what size the person's gift or how extensive his or her activity. Epaphroditus was someone placing himself at the disposal of another for the "work of Christ" (2:6-7). He risked his life *while participating* in the gospel. Like a nurse who risks his or her life by treating the sick and diseased, Epaphroditus put his life at risk. A true disciple of Jesus Christ resolves to put the mission above all else, even life itself.

There is no indication that Epaphroditus knew *before* his journey to Rome that he would experience a life-threatening illness. But at the least he resolved to participate and persevere in the work of Christ. There was understood risk in what he set out to do. So with us. We must resolve to be faithful and obedient Christians—even at the risk of life itself (2:8, 12).

Final Resolve: To Correct a Self-centered Church by Citing Two Models of Sacrifice

Paul continues his letter with two missionary stories. He tells them in order to inform the Philippians of his situation and intentions. But they also provide flesh-and-blood examples— models—of what it means to live the Christ-life. In essence Paul is saying, "To correct your self-interest and restore your joy, honor these men and emulate their attitudes."

Paul would send Timothy to Philippi "as soon as I see how things go with me" (2:23). But he would send Epaphroditus at once. Both would address the problems Paul perceived in the congregation.

The gist of the Timothy-Epaphroditus references in 2:19-30 was to make clear that the welfare of the Church was at issue. Timothy and Epaphroditus had given their lives (Epaphroditus almost literally!) for the sake of the gospel. Epaphroditus showed his commitment by conveying the Philippians' love-offering (4:10ff.). Timothy showed his through his partnership with Paul.

There are other indicators that suggest Paul is creating a tone, an ethos, through the telling of these stores. Epaphroditus *longed* for his home church (2:26; cf. 1:8 and 2 Corinthians 5:2; 9:14). He was *distressed* that the Philippians had heard he was ill (2:26; Jesus' anguish in Gethsemane, Matthew 26:37; Mark 14:33). Epaphroditus had a deep emotional attachment to the Philippian church. These words indicate he was deeply concerned over the church's condition.

Again, we hear from Paul: "I am all the more eager to send him, so that when you see him again you may be glad and I may have less anxiety" (Philippians 2:28; see also 2:19). Paul faced injustice as a prisoner of Rome.[15] The company of these two associates was sweet. But he too was willing to sacrifice companionship for the sake of the Philippian church. Certainly he was hoping the Philippians would respond like this: "Paul is right. Let's place concern for the church and the gospel above all else. Let us share in the sacrifice that Paul, Timothy and Epaphroditus have made for the sake of the church and its mission."

Timothy and Epaphroditus were to be honored. Paul writes: "Welcome [Epaphroditus] in the Lord with great joy, and honor men like him [and Timothy]" (2:29). While we continue to honor sacrifice, we more typically honor those who succeed. It is the successful whom we seek to emulate. We prize the rugged individualism that pervades our culture.

How Do We Qualify for Honor?

How do we qualify as men and women to be "honored"? It is an important question. Our answer, ultimately, will affect the Church. The Church *is* the issue in Philippians! Timothy and Epaphroditus had passed the test. They had risked their lives for the *work of Christ* (2:30). We prove ourselves as honorable Christians by submitting to the authority of another more experienced Christian. We prove ourselves by losing our lives for the sake of the gospel. And such resolve will mean the potential for loss—whether it be loss of life, material goods or lifestyle.

The Church is in need of those who will sacrifice for their own local assemblies. The problem is that Christians succumb to the cultural temptation to put their needs above the needs of others. This is only amplified by the fact that each congregation operates on a volunteer basis. But Christianity and Church life are not options. Until we understand that, we will never risk our careers, our homes, our goods, our reputations, our North American fulfillment, or ourselves. And the unsaved and the unchurched will continue to perceive the gospel as an option among competing "lifestyles." We cannot expect that the unchurched will place a high value on what we consider cheap.

We like to sing Luther's "A Mighty Fortress Is Our

God." Perhaps we would do well to actually believe the final stanza:

> That Word above all earthy powers,
>   No thanks to them, abideth;
> The Spirit and the gifts are ours
>   Through Him who with us sideth.

Notice the words that follow:

> Let goods and kindred go,
>   This mortal life also;
> The body they may kill:
>   God's truth abideth still,
>   His kingdom is forever.

Just perhaps God is looking yet today for men and women who will put the Church first. Perhaps He is yet looking for men and women who, while they live, will resolve to live with all their might. Who knows? God brought about a great awakening the last time someone made that resolve. Perhaps He will do it again. We should pray like Billy Graham, who once cried out to God:

> Lord, do it again. Do what You did when the apostles were called. Do what You did following Pentecost. Do what You did with Saul of Tarsus, Augustine, Luther, Calvin, John Wesley, George Whitefield and William Booth. Lord, do it again! And help us reach the world for Jesus Christ.

Endnotes
[1] Henry Rogers, *The Works of Jonathan Edwards,* Vol. I, revised by Edward Hickman (London: Ball, Arnold and

Co., 1840), lxii-lxiv.

[2] In the preface of his translation of the Book of Acts, *The Young Church in Action* (1955).

[3] For further New Testament references to Timothy see Acts 16; Romans 16:21; 1 Corinthians 4:17; 16:10; 2 Corinthians 1:1; Philippians 1:1; 1 Thessalonians 1:1; 2 Thessalonians 1:1; Philemon 1 as well as the two letters to Timothy.

[4] Epaphroditus was sent first in order to carry the letter. Timothy would soon follow in order to correct the matters about which Paul wrote and then report back.

[5] Note: *Iso,* "like," "equal to"; *psychon,* "soul." See Gerald F. Hawthorne, *Word Biblical Commentary,* Vol. 43, *Philippians* (Waco, TX: Word, 1983), 109.

[6] Paul's constant use of "to think" (*phronein/phroneo*) highlights his insistence that there is a proper "mind" to have regarding the Church and the work of the Church. (See 1:7; 2:2, 5; 3:15, 19; 4:2, 10.)

[7] Normally this word is used throughout the New Testament to indicate worry or anxiety, a mood or attitude that should not characterize the Christian (Matthew 13:22; Mark 4:19; Luke 8:14; 21:34; 1 Peter 5:7 and even in Philippians 4:6).

[8] See Paul Johnson, *Intellectuals* (New York: Harper & Row, 1990) for an insightful biography on the great minds that have shaped the modern world. I fear our Christian rhetoric is often just a Christianized rephrasing of modern libertarians who habitually forget that people matter more than concepts and vague rationales.

[9] "Character" is the NIV's rendering in Romans 5:4 of *dokime,* meaning "proof," "tested."

[10] See chapter 6.

[11] Hawthorne, 25.

[12] Romans 1:1; 1 Corinthians 1:1; 9:1, 2, 5; 12:28, 29; 2 Corinthians 1:1; 11:5.

[13] Hawthorne, 116-117.

[14] *Theological Dictionary of the New Testament,* Vol. 4, G.

Kittel and G. Friedrich, eds. (Grand Rapids, MI: Eerdmans, 1964-76), 219-222.

[15] The reference to "sorrow upon sorrow" (2:27) probably means that Paul already suffers from house arrest, but God did not allow further suffering by the loss of this faithful servant, Epaphroditus.

CHAPTER 9

Discerning Between Christ and Rubbish
Philippians 3:1-11

LIFE'S LESSONS OFTEN COME FROM MOST unusual sources. For me, one such lesson came during a driver education session. I was sixteen. And it was not a good session.

It was spring, 1974. On a winding New Hampshire road, traffic was backed up behind me for at least a mile. Apparently, I was driving too slowly. Eventually the instructor found a safe place for me to pull over. The car immediately behind us pulled over as well. Not a good sign.

The driver didn't even look at me. With noticeable frustration and anger he directed his comments to my instructor. "If the guy can't drive, get him off the road!"

The irate motorist returned to his car and the line of traffic continued to file by. I was mortified. My emotions must have registered on my face.

"Relax," the instructor said to me; "we'll get back to

driving in a moment." Right then I wasn't sure I wanted to drive—ever!

The instructor gave me time to settle down. Finally he asked, "You know what your problem is?"

Yeah, I thought to myself, *I can't drive!*

"You are concerned about staying between the yellow center line and the white side line," the instructor continued. "As a result, you drive too slowly and weave back and forth. You are concentrating on the road right in front of you. Try this: Look where you want to be going."

Look where you want to be going. Good advice. It helped me through driver education and to be a reasonably safe driver ever since. It's also good advice for contemporary North American Christians.

Our culture tends to make us overly concerned about the road immediately in front of us. Everything from TV sitcoms that solve problems in thirty minutes to fast-food restaurants and instant-cash machines put pressure on us. They force us to define ourselves by how we respond to and feel about the immediate—the temporal.

Where the Letter to the Philippians Is Going
Paul moves from a context oriented toward his relationship with the Philippian congregation (1:3-2:30) to a section that is deeply theological (3:1-11). We have seen the models of servanthood that occupied his attention: Christ (2:5-11), Timothy (2:19-24), Epaphroditus (2:25-30). He even refers to his own example (2:17-18). Now Paul returns to how his own life relates to the gospel, but with a theologically enriched vocabulary.

He has already discussed church disunity and joylessness at Philippi in relation to the church's interaction with the world surrounding it (1:27-30). He has discussed as well the individual member's relationship to the local body of Christ (2:1-4). Now he lifts these issues into the realm of the nature of the gospel itself. The congregation in Philippi must grapple with their lack of persevering joy in relation to the essentials of the faith: the death and resurrection of Jesus Christ (3:10-11).

The pressures of life and the false teachings infiltrating the congregation stole the members' joy and diminished their ability to persevere. Our own moment in time places certain pressures on our churches and on us. There is temptation to accommodate ourselves with the status quo, to identify with the hedonistic culture around us. We want to feel comfortable in modernity. We dislike feeling alienated from our surrounding culture, from our democracy. But if we succumb, we too will be robbed of our persevering joy— and the power of true Christian identity.

We must place our confidence not in the world or the things of the world (1 John 2:15-17; Romans 12:1-2) but in the essentials of our faith: the cross and the resurrection. Only in doing so can we restore our identity. Only in doing so will the Church be able to persevere amid the tensions of life.

Rejoice in the Lord

A wise Christian once made an interesting observation: For the unbeliever, joy is peripheral and suffering is fundamental; but for the believer, suffering is peripheral and joy is fundamental. Why is that true? For the unbeliever, the peripheral issues are answered and the fundamental ones are left unanswered. But for the Christian, the fundamental questions of life are answered and the peripheral ones are unanswered.

Regrettably, the Christian community has lost this basic perspective. We have lost our joy because we have switched the poles of our existence. We have succumbed to our culture's fascination with the now, the immediate. As a result, we are preoccupied with the peripheral issues of life, forgetting the essentials. And this causes us to define both our Christian and church identities by the peripheral issues we face rather than by the eternal, fundamental realities of Christ's death and resurrection.

Repeatedly Paul expresses his own sense of joy. Repeatedly he asks the Philippians to share in his joy (Philippians 1:4, 18, 25-26; 2:2, 18, 29; 3:1; 4:4, 10). Now again he appeals to the Philippians to rejoice: "Finally, my brothers, rejoice in the Lord! It is no trouble for me to write the same things to you again, and it is a safeguard for you" (3:1). If only the Philippians would share in Paul's joy, they would restore the attitude that brings health to the church and confidence to the congregation.

The text that follows (3:2-11) refocuses the Christian community's attention on the essential, fundamental aspects of the faith: the cross and the resurrection. Typically this text is viewed within a works-versus-faith context, reminding us that our righteousness before God is worthless if it comes from anything else but faith in the finished work of Christ. Although this is quite true, it stops short of Paul's fuller intentions for the Philippians—and for us later readers of his letter.

Some Form of Judaizing Had Infiltrated the Church

Some form of Judaizing had taken place in Philippi. Some of the Philippian believers—possibly some of the leaders (cf. 1:1)—had become enamored with works-righteousness. But why would a church primarily comprised of Gentiles in a very Gentile city find Torah observance and circumcision appealing?

The answer is as much sociological as theological. To suggest that the Gentile Philippian believers were attracted to Torah observance just because of pride is to miss the bigger problem. The church's reorientation toward a Judaized Christianity can better be explained by the church's loss of social standing. Simply put, they were going through an identity crisis. The congregation was in a severe clash between society and the Church.[1]

Philippians 3:2-11 fits neatly into Paul's monologue regarding the issue of Christian citizenship. Note Paul's use of two words at the beginning of what he has to say about Christian citizenship—*polteuesthe* and *stekete,* translated "conduct yourselves" and "stand firm" (1:27). Then in 3:20 and 4:1 he employs very similar language—*politeuma* and *stekete* translated "citizenship" and (again) "stand firm." He uses the words almost as "bookends" to include what he has to say about Christian citizenship.

In 3:1, Paul says he is writing concerning the "same things." So the issue is still that of walking worthy of the gospel of Christ (1:27; see my earlier commentary in chapter 4 on that verse). In fact, he said it is a safeguard (*asphale*) for them to hear it again. Elsewhere the word is used to denote security, an anchor, to be steadfast (Acts 21:34; 22:30; 25:26; Hebrews 6:19). Christianity defined by the person of Jesus Christ brings security to the Christian's life. Judaism—or anything else used to define the Christian life—is a false security.[2]

Why Would Judaism Attract Philippian Christians?

But why would the believers at Philippi put their freedom in Christ at risk? Although we will get to the details of the text, it is important to understand that Paul was attempting to discuss their identity as Christians. He writes that they, not those who teach circumcision, are the people of God (Philippians 3:2-3). The false teachers were most likely suggesting "that the Philippians' present status as Christians was incomplete or valueless."[3] Thus the agitators were able to use the Philippians' crisis of culture to lure them to a seemingly more secure basis for their faith. This led to a false security both with the Roman culture and with God.

The church at Philippi faced a real conflict with Roman law and custom (see Introduction). In Roman law the Jewish sect found a measure of toleration and protection. In fact Judaism was called *religio licita* (a legitimate religion). The Jewish community was free from certain offensive civic obligations, the imperial cult functions and worshipping of Roman deities. In Philippi, a city known for its high regard for Caesar, Christians were especially at risk. In Philippi the Christian sect was *religio illicita* (an illegitimate religion) because it was antithetical to the imperial cult and the worship of Caesar as Lord. The false, Judaistic teaching seemed helpful because it would ease the conflict with Rome. It would give the Christians a legitimate social identity and a measure of protection.

Paul's text here is surprisingly applicable to North American Christians today. Our gospel is at odds with contemporary culture. Yet we love our culture. We enjoy our citizenship. And we trust that the structures of our culture—the tax-exempt laws, the media, technology, freedom of expression, freedom of travel, upward mobility, educational and business opportunities, government—will enable us both to continue our church life and, at the same time, enjoy our democratic freedoms. Is it any surprise that North American Christians today are so filled with anxiety? We are defining our church life and our personal spirituality by our culture. This has robbed us of our persevering joy.

Paul says to the Philippians: "Rejoice in the Lord!" (3:1). He will repeat the admonition later. Then Paul cites his personal testimony to bolster confidence among them (3:2-11). If we imitate Paul's attitude and his confidence in the essentials of the faith, we will find our own Christian confidence restored.

Watch Those Identity Symbols
Symbols give meaning and order to our lives. The flag, a

wedding ring, a gang jacket, in the United States the Republican elephant can call up certain behavioral patterns, certain commitments. Social scientists and anthropologists, in the words of Robert Wuthnow,

> generally conceive of religion as a system of symbols that evoke a sense of holistic or transcendent meaning ...Symbols are acts, objects, utterances or events that stand for something—that is, they give meaning to something by connecting it to something else.[4]

They give meaning to an individual or a community by connecting the person or community to something or someone beyond, someone on the outside. The more we find meaning in earthly symbols, the more we will foster in ourselves elements of pride and status. And the more we will diminish our persevering joy.

Paul has been relatively calm, like a mother caring for her child or a nurse tending an invalid. Now, in 3:2, exhortation makes way for warning. The NIV expresses the warning but once: *"Watch out."* Actually, Paul says it three times: "Watch out for those dogs, watch out for those men who do evil, watch out for those mutilators of the flesh" (3:2, free translation). The warning is harsh. Paul's tone is harsh. His words are calculated and biting.

The father of the Philippian church chooses words that have even a harsh sound. He wants to gain their attention quickly. His words describing the false teachers and the agitators have the rough *k* sound: *kunas* (dogs); *kakous ergatas* (evil workers), *katatomen* (mutilators). In each case he inverts a Jewish boast. *Dogs* refers to those outside the covenant (Matthew 7:6; 15:26-27). It was a dirty slang word used by Jews for Gentiles. *Evil workers* was a play on a common Jewish and Christian term for missionary. Thus reversing a positive title to indicate that those who had come into their midst were actually workers of evil rather than faithful bearers of the gospel (2 Corinthians 11:13; also see 1 Corinthians 3:13-15; 9:6; 1 Timothy 5:18; 2 Timothy 2:15 and Matthew 9:38).

God's True People

Paul's last epithet, *mutilators,* was also a wordplay regarding circumcision. Literally *katatomen* refers to the pagan ritual of cutting themselves. Jews considered this an abomination. Paul assures the Christian community in Philippi that they are the true circumcision, the true people of God. He accuses the Judaizers of being counterfeits who actually just mutilate the flesh.

Paul's warning comes deadly quick for those contemplating Judaism as a safe haven for the Christian community against the Roman juggernaut. But the affirmation is equally poignant: "For it is we who are the circumcision, we who worship by the Spirit of God, who glory in Christ Jesus, and who put no confidence in the flesh" (3:3). The indicative statement is simple: "*We*—both believing Jews like myself and believing Gentiles like yourselves— are the true circumcision, and we do not need any fleshly mutilation to prove who we are. *We* do not put confidence in the flesh; we trust in Christ Jesus the Lord" (see also Ephesians 2:8-10, 11-13; Romans 2:28-29; 8:1-4).

Circumcision was the old covenant's symbol of identity, the prerequisite for membership in the people of God. Since Christ has come, however, God's people are marked by the Holy Spirit and Christ's work of redemption. Paul follows with three phrases to reinforce his assertion. The Christian's identity is not in works of the flesh (whether for the pride of status or social protection) but in God's provision.

The Christian Community's Three Identifying Marks

One, the Christian community *worships by the Spirit of God.* Obviously this contrasts with the Law-centered (Torah-centered) Judaizers (Romans 2:29; 2 Corinthians 3:6). Paul's reference to the Spirit indicates the true abiding sign or identity marker for those in relationship to God (Romans 8:1-4). But this designation also indicates that God is the initiator of our worship, not we. Even in worship we depend on God—not the external rituals and identity markers of the older covenant (or the social structures of our own culture!). The word *worship* is most likely a veiled reference to the Old Testament Levitical temple service. In stark contrast to the "mutilators," the Christian community serves God by the power of the Spirit (2 Corinthians 3:6).

Two, the Christian community *glories in Christ Jesus.* The idea of *glory* is literally "to boast," that is, to place one's full confidence and trust in Christ Jesus (1 Corinthians 1:31; 2 Corinthians 10:17; Jeremiah 9:24; Galatians 6:14). The Christian community's identity is based not on external symbols (for example, circumcision, or the national flag) but in the person of Jesus Christ. Our Christian identity neither consists of cultural structures nor rests upon human agencies.

Paul's third phrase describing how the true people of God are identified underscores what is actually robbing the Philippian Christians of their persevering joy. We, the true community of God, Paul says, *do not put confidence in the flesh.* This, too, is an obvious reference to circumcision. But there is more. Paul sees irony in that term *flesh.*

The Philippians were being lured into thinking that their faith *in Christ* was not enough to fully qualify as "sons of God" (Galatians 3-4). They saw themselves as vulnerable. As Christians, they had lost social acceptance. Their place "in the world" was diminished, and they lacked a sense of communal security. Why else would Gentiles submit to the Jewish rite of circumcision? By doing so they could lessen their tension with Rome. Roman culture had placed them on the periphery. Circumcision would bring them into the social orbit.

Beware a False Security

But Paul warns that it would be a false security. Identifying with the Judaizers would give the Philippians a measure of relief as to their place in society—temporarily. But the issue of their true identity was a matter of eternal weight. Trusting in *the flesh* (whether an earthly institution or in one's natural abilities or achievements) aligned them with the world rather than with Christ. And that was the issue. Paul is about to demonstrate, through his own testimony (Philippians 3:4-14), that there is no future in Judaism *or in any earthly, human resource.* He writes:

> *If anyone else thinks he has reasons to put confidence in the flesh, I have more: circumcised on the eighth day, of the people of Israel, of the tribe of Benjamin, a Hebrew of Hebrews; in regard to the law, a Pharisee; as for zeal, persecuting the church; as for legalistic righteousness, faultless.* (3:4-6)

Paul does not deny the advantage that his heritage and previous activity as a faithful Jew gave him. He could have such "confidence in the flesh." He was an Israelite par excellence. He was fully Jewish from birth, born into a noble tribe. Both his parents were Israelites.[5] The exercise of his Jewish obedience was beyond reproach. If there ever was an Israelite who could claim confidence and social, as well as, religious security, Paul was that one.

Paul's Own Enviable Record

Notice what Paul says about his own record: "In regard to the law, a Pharisee; as for zeal, persecuting the church; as for legalistic righteousness, faultless."[6] Paul's past accolades as a Hebrew and a member of the Pharisaic Jewish community might have put him—temporarily—in a socially acceptable "religion," safe from Roman law and custom. But such a place also put him at odds with the gospel—and at odds with the true Lord of the earth, Jesus Christ.

Paul was the quintessential Judaizer. He was a Pharisee. The keeping of the Law had led him not to join the Church but to destroy it (1 Corinthians 15:9; Acts 22:2-5; 26:9-11; 1 Timothy 1:13). And such a life of Law-observance declared that Paul was faultlessly righteous.[7] Now, in the face of Christ, the Israelite of Israelites writes: "But whatever was to my profit I now consider loss for the sake of Christ" (Philippians 3:7).

Paul's use of the past tense and perfect voice signifies that the things he considered a loss when he met Christ he still considers a loss.[8] He is still warning against any notion that Jewish identity symbols help anyone's relationship with God. Neither are they a comfort in Roman society. At one time Paul considered those things "profit." But in the light of Christ and His redemption, he reckons those former profits as a loss.[9]

Interestingly, Jesus in the Gospels sets forth a similar "mind" for Christian discipleship. He said, "If anyone would come after me, he must deny himself and take up his cross and follow me" (Matthew 16:24; Mark 8:34; see also Luke 9:23). Jesus went on to explain this new concept of gaining and losing:

> *Whoever wants to save his life will lose it,*
> *but whoever loses his life for me will find it.*
> *What good will it be for a man if he gains the*

whole world, yet forfeits his soul? (Matthew 16:25-26)[10]

These words of our Lord parallel Paul's instruction to the Philippians. As one commentator has said, "As long as a man keeps thinking of his personal advantages, inherited or acquired, as giving him a better standing before God, all such things are disadvantages to him."[11]

Knowing Jesus as Lord Restores Corporate Confidence

There seems to be a lack of confidence and persevering joy throughout much of the Church in North America today. I believe there are two simple reasons for this. One, we have accommodated ourselves to our culture. Two, we have privatized our faith. When the issues facing the Church are social and cultural, we do not discuss sanctification. That's because much of our view of sanctification is also privatized and clothed in cultural garb.

Throughout Philippians 1 and 2, Paul has been calling for a more sanctified life—personally and corporately. We too often relate sanctification to moral issues and to sin (in the private sphere of an individual Christian) rather than to social issues or structures that affect the life of the Church. But Paul moves us into this very pertinent realm where sanctification must be realized. The issue in every aspect of sanctification is *knowing Christ as Lord*—personally and corporately.

Sanctification is three-sided. The Christian is sanctified *positionally* "in Christ" (1 Corinthians 1:2; Hebrews 10:10). Because Christians live in time and are not perfected at conversion, we are also subject to the pains of growing in Christ (2 Peter 3:17-18; Romans 8:18-30). Because of this we are exhorted by the New Testament writers *to be* sanctified. Although there are many ways this sanctifying event is described, it is when we truly enthrone

Jesus Christ as Lord, not just in principle but in fact, that sanctification becomes progressive, moving the Christian toward more Christlikeness. Philippians 3:7-8 is a paragon of a text describing this process.

There is no doubt that Paul is addressing Christians at Philippi. They are "separated unto God," sanctified "in Christ" (1:1; 1:29). Yet the Philippians are *in crisis.* They have come to a place where they must put themselves—no matter what the social consequences—under the lordship of Christ. Like Paul (3:7), they had once considered the claims of Christ (Acts 16:15, 31) and received Him (which began their conflict with Rome). Now they must recognize that the *crisis* they face—their identity crisis—presents a choice between Caesar or Jesus (Philippians 3:8; 1:27ff.). Will Caesar be Lord, or Jesus?

A Significant Change of Verb Tenses

Paul adds: "What is more, I consider everything a loss compared to the surpassing greatness of knowing Christ Jesus my Lord" (3:8). Paul makes a significant change of verb tenses. In 3:7 Paul indicates a past decision he had made about Christ Jesus the Lord. In 3:8 he uses the word *consider* (*count,* KJV, NASB; *deem, reckon*) in the present tense to indicate that he continues to consider Jesus as his Lord. It is as if Paul is saying, "The decision I made at my conversion was no mistake. Even now I continue to count all things to be loss in view of knowing Jesus as Lord." The Philippians must likewise make that decision in the face of *their* crisis.

Paul renounces any *profit* that Torah observance had for him (3:3-6). He broadens the renunciation beyond Judaism to include *everything* (3:8). Everything in the present age that is of value for deriving identity and/or social acceptance is *rubbish* when compared with *knowing Christ.* For the Philippians, anything a Gentile might find tempting to rely on as a sign of acceptability to God or society is to be considered *a loss.*[12]

The primary issue here is *knowing Christ Jesus as Lord.* The apostle refers to the Old Testament idea of "knowing" God and applies it to Jesus. Throughout the Old Testament when God addressed Israel He often began by saying, "I am the Lord your God, who brought you out of Egypt" (Exodus 20:2). At other times God said He would act "that you may know that I am the Lord" (Exodus 10:2). God established Himself as Lord over against all other gods that surrounded Israel. And Israel was to experience and know personally that He, Yahweh, is the Lord God. Thus the essence of knowing God is a personal (and community) experience of meeting God as Lord.

"Knowing" Christ refers to a personal acquaintance with Him as Lord.[13] This is the "surpassing greatness" compared with whom all else is valueless. The idea of "knowing" here does not denote a body of information concerning Christ Jesus (that is, knowing *about* Christ). Through his testimony Paul appeals to the Philippians to not trade their personal acquaintance with the Lord Jesus for anything lesser (cf. Romans 1:22-23; Matthew 13:44-46).

This Is Significant to Our Sanctification

All of this is significant to our sanctification. Always sanctification is related to the lordship of Jesus. This fact is especially important to the Philippian context.

To understand Paul's words here, we must more fully understand his conversion to Christ—the Damascus Road event. Luke chronicles the confrontation in Acts 9. Twice more he records Paul's own telling of it (Acts 22:1-21; 26:1-23).[14]

Paul was on his way to Damascus to kill or arrest Jewish followers of the Way. He was not interested in Gentiles who had become Christians. He only sought Jews who had accepted Jesus as the Messiah. As far as he was concerned, they were the traitors to Israel—and to God. After all, Jesus had been crucified. God's Messiah would never allow Himself to be cursed by hanging from a tree (Deuteronomy 21:23).

Picture, then, Paul upon a donkey, moving along the Damascus Road. He was the faithful, righteous, obedient servant of God. He was in the right. Jesus was the Impostor, and the Jews who followed Him were blaspheming God's name. Then came the blinding light, literally knocking Paul off his beast to the ground. And the Voice: "Saul, Saul, why do you persecute me?" (Acts 9:4).

"Who are you, Lord?" Paul asks (Acts 9:5). Paul understood from his knowledge of the Old Testament what a heavenly vision was. He knew God was revealing Himself. Very soon it became all too clear that Jesus, the very One whose followers Paul had been persecuting, was speaking. Paul knew that a day of resurrection would come. And on that day God would vindicate His faithful servants. So here was Jesus, resurrected! That could mean only one thing: Jesus was God's Messiah. Jesus was Lord (Acts 2:24, 36).

Paul faced a major dilemma. Paul had been wrong. Jesus was who He claimed to be. Jesus was right and righteous. Paul was unrighteous. It was a pivotal point for him. Conversion is an understanding that Jesus is Lord, the Messiah. This is the *profit*—the *gain* compared with which all else is *rubbish*. At that moment, the Damascus Road event put Paul at odds with Judaism *and* with Roman culture.

The lordship of Christ is no small matter. As it put Saul the persecutor in tension with Judaism, so the Lordship of Christ puts the Church in tension with society and culture. When Paul preached the gospel in Philippi for the first time, he made clear the centrality of Jesus as Lord (Acts 16:18, 31-32). No doubt this was an implicit attack on the emperor. Paul was arrested for espousing anti-Caesar ideas (Acts 16:19-24). Right from the start, the gospel put the Philippian church at odds with their surrounding culture. These Roman citizens were attaching themselves to a rival Caesar.

Jesus, Not Caesar, Is Lord

Philippians is explicitly a document reminding the Church that Jesus is Lord. *Kurios,* the Greek word for *Lord,* is used fifteen times in this short letter.[15] Paul refers to Jesus as his personal Lord (3:8; 2:19, 24; 4:10). Jesus is Lord of the Church (1:2; 3:1; 4:1, 23). And with an explicitly anti-Caesar tone, he refers to Jesus as the Lord of the universe, the cosmos (2:10-11; 3:2-21). Paul calls Jesus equal to God, *isa theo* (2:6). It is interesting that one of Caesar's own titles was *isotheos,* "equal to the gods." In fact, to pay honor to Caesar was to pay honor to a god, for the imperial cult of Rome itself described Caesar as *isotheoi timai* (honors equivalent paid to the gods).[16]

Paul considered the benefits of Roman society and the privileges of his heritage "rubbish." Paul uses the word *skubalon.* The KJV rendering—*dung*—is inelegant, but it may come closest to both the meaning and the impact of the Greek word itself. It was an offensive expression. It was the manure you stepped on in the streets, the refuse thrown out to the dogs, the excrement burned in heaps beyond the city gates.

With emotional and rhetorical expertise, Paul makes his point. Knowing Christ is infinitely beyond any other possible benefit or achievement. By contrast, Judaism's storied traditions and Caesar's cultural structures are no more than foul-smelling garbage. The same may be said for our democracy and religious freedom. We must be able to discern between Christ and rubbish.

We gain Christ at the risk of losing everything else. We give ourselves to the lordship of Jesus Christ without reserve in order to "gain Christ and be found in him, not having a righteousness of [our] own...but that which is through faith in Christ—the righteousness that comes from God and is by faith" (3:8-9).

Being "found in him" explains what it means to gain Christ.[17] The Philippians' joy (or the lack of it) was conditioned upon where they placed their eternal confidence. Paul used the idea of being found to indicate both a present and a future position for the believer. On the one hand, *being found* is a judicial term indicating the judgment rendered at a trial ("The defendant was found not guilty.") Already Paul has set the conversation within the context of the "final day" (1:6, 10; 2:16; 3:20-21). Counting on a righteousness based on the observance of Judaism's Torah would nullify the work of Christ (Galatians 2:21) and contradict a person's "knowing Christ Jesus [as] Lord." The only eternal security is "being found in him" on that final day when God renders accounts to everyone (Romans 2:6; Psalm 62:12; Proverbs 24:12; Ecclesiastes 12:14).

"We do not buy love, but we owe it everything"

On the other hand, "being found in him" involves our present position as God's people. The idea of righteousness here points to a relationship with Yahweh God rather than simply a moral code or religious observance. The word group (in both Hebrew and Greek) from which *righteousness* is derived is broad in its range of meaning. But the context here points to a righteousness that God confers on an individual (or community) as His own possession. Which brings us back to identity symbols. What identity symbol will determine a person's "righteous" relationship to God?[18]

The Philippians context suggests that Paul implies two things when he states that he desires a righteousness based not on Torah-keeping but on Jesus Christ. First, trusting in the Torah as an identity symbol for a relationship to

God would be at odds with the fulfillment of the covenant by Jesus Christ. Second, simply suggesting that our righteousness can come from Torah observance—that is, from works (Ephesians 2:8-9)—trivializes righteousness. Such a works orientation eventuates in pride, and pride leads to disunity. Inevitably, a controlling elite would determine who was and who was not spiritual. Status, rather than humility and servanthood, would become a spiritual pursuit. Such a works righteousness would continue to divide the congregation. It would perpetuate the congregation's false sense of security.

The righteousness that comes through Jesus Christ by faith renders the recipient humble before God and fellow human beings. Like the man who found treasure hidden in a field (Matthew 13:44), we sell all we have to gain that treasure. Like the merchant who discovers the pearl of great price, we sell everything to buy it (Matthew 13:45-46). Although our faith should produce good works (Ephesians 2:10; James 2:14-18), the issue is on what we base our Christian identity. Ultimately, each individual Christian and the Christian community as a whole must find existence and identity in knowing Christ Jesus as Lord. Nothing less is adequate.

"We do not buy love," Calvin Miller writes, "but we owe it everything."[19]

Embracing the Work of Christ Produces Personal Confidence

In the NIV, Philippians 3:10-11 is an independent sentence. But it is also the culmination of gaining Christ and being found in Him (3:8-9).[20] "Knowing Christ Jesus my Lord" is the sanctified life. To know Jesus as Lord means also to know "the power of his resurrection and the fellowship of sharing in his sufferings, becoming like him in his death" (3:10).[21]

Pivotal events so often determine a community's or an individual's identity. And that identity often determines how a community or an individual relates to the rest of the world. The Israelites defined themselves by the Red Sea crossing. That event determined who they belonged to and how they related to the nations around them. They were the people of Yahweh God. They were to serve and glorify the Creator-God of the universe. So in American history, the Declaration of Independence produced a new identity for many of those who settled the New World. Americans defined themselves by the constitution they forged. They related to the rest of the world as children of the constitution.

Similarly, the defining event for the Christian and the Christian community is the resurrection of Jesus Christ. The resurrection of Jesus ushered into time and space the beginning of God's rule and reign. The power of the resurrection lies not in some explosive-generating ability to perform the Christian life; it *is* the Christian life. It offers a new focus, one that defines life not by worldly terms or structures. The world is destined to pass away, but God's eternal life transcends mortal life. Those who follow the resurrected Jesus Christ will know the power of His resurrection. It alone explains the fundamental and essential issues of life. Jesus' resurrection proves that God is all-powerful and that He keeps His word. It is evidence that mortal life is not the true measure of things.

In his book *Can Man Live Without God?*, Ravi Zacharias points out that man is always attempting to find significance:

> Pascal knew whereof he spoke when he said
> that he had learned to define life backwards
> and live it forwards. By that he meant that he
> first defined death and then his life accord-
> ingly...The resurrection of Christ informs

suffering, and that is why the existence of God
and the confidence of hope go together.[22]

Status and pride as well as the temporal structures of
the world are no longer the measure of our significance.

The Fellowship of Sharing in Christ's Sufferings

Another goal of knowing Christ is "the fellowship of sharing in his sufferings." This is not simply a reference to sharing in Christ's death (Romans 6:1-5; Ephesians 2:6). Paul's
intentions go beyond such positional truth. Frequently Paul
portrays the lot of believers as a life of sharing in Christ's
sufferings (1 Thessalonians 1:6; 3:2-3; 2 Corinthians 1:5;
4:7-18; Romans 8:17; Colossians 1:24; Philippians 1:29).

We must not lose sight of the central issue
confronting this congregation. By accepting the gospel of
Christ the Philippians had become alienated from society.
To relieve the tension, they were in process of adopting a
more Jewish version of Christianity, something Rome
would tolerate. But any accommodation, whether the
symbols were Jewish or Roman, was a compromise offensive to the true Lord of the Universe. Any sense of security
felt by the congregation was false.

The resurrection is the Church's new symbol of
identity. But the Church must understand that sharing in the
resurrection means sharing in the suffering and the death
that preceded the resurrection. That is why the Christian and
the Christian community is to share in Christ's suffering.
Our goal is "becoming like [Christ] in his death."

Suffering is the path to God's kingdom. Christ's own
life affirms it. In 2:6-8 we learned that Christ did not count
His equality with God as something to be selfishly
grasped—for His own advantage. The reference to the cross
there and here in 3:10 would have been offensive to Roman
citizens. Dying on a cross was appalling in the extreme. One

of their own writers remarked: "Let the very name of the cross be far away not only from the body of a Roman citizen but even from his thoughts, his eyes, his ears."[23] Going to a cross as a means of gaining power was in radical contrast with the Roman way to power. Christ did not grab for power. It came through service, through giving—and in dying.[24]

When Paul climaxes his thought in 3:11, we discover a humble rather than an arrogant believer: "and so, somehow, to attain to the resurrection from the dead." At first we might ask: *Is Paul suggesting that his own resurrection in not a certainty?* Other texts (Romans 8; 1 Corinthians 15) leave us in no doubt that Paul expected to be resurrected. Paul's seeming uncertainty in Philippians 3:11 is in fact a rhetorical device he uses to instill humility in a prideful congregation.

Paul is indicating that God will vindicate the person who determines to know Christ Jesus as Lord (2:9-11; 1:28). For a time we may be at odds with a society antithetical toward Christ and the gospel. For a time we may feel uncomfortable and even foolish. But a time will come when God will confirm that we were on the right track after all. Like our Lord, we too will attain to the resurrection from the dead.

Do You Know the Difference?
True security comes in discerning between Christ Jesus and rubbish. How much of our Christian life reflects a biblical, Christ-centered walk? How much of it depends on our society's cultural venue? Someone has said he who marries the spirit of the age soon finds himself a widower. For the Christian community, the statement is truer yet. If our North American governments were suddenly to tax churches as they do businesses, how many would survive?

Today the church is in an identity crisis. On the one hand, we are uncomfortable with the raging immorality and evil on all sides. We are distrustful of government seemingly running rampant. On the other hand, we enjoy our democratic freedoms and our favored status. We forget that these freedoms have a price. Yet we continue to accommodate ourselves to our culture—through our lifestyles, by how we want church to be, in what we expect God to do for us.

In his book *Beyond Cultural Wars* Michael Horton outlines modern Christendom's fascination with contemporary culture at the expense of biblical orthodoxy, spiritual life and church life. "Even the formulas evangelicals create for serving the Lord," Horton observes, "...are geared toward self-fulfillment." He cites the dominant secular, individualistic values of the United States: materialism, competition, achievement, success. From these, he says, we create our beliefs, our attitudes, our definition of reality.[25]

The Philippians were hoping to accommodate to Roman culture by trading the essentials of Christianity for values Rome would tolerate. Less than three centuries later, the Roman Empire and the Christian Church in the empire merged. And when Rome finally caved in to the barbarians, Jerome made this sad comment: "What is to become of the Church now that Rome has fallen?"

Let us not be fooled. It is a false security to go with the tide of cultural comfort. The more we accommodate to the culture surrounding us, the more estranged from God we will be. When the structures of North American life are overrun by the barbarians, what will become of the church?

Persevering joy can be restored to the Church. It comes not by power borrowed from democratic vote and democratic freedoms, but by way of the resurrection. It comes by participating in the sufferings of Christ. It comes by knowing Christ Jesus as Lord.

G.K. Chesterton once remarked, "We do not want a religion that is right where we are right. What we want is a religion that is right where we are wrong." It is either Christ or rubbish. For the Church—and for the individual

Christian—there is no in-between.

Endnotes
[1] Mikael Tellbe, "The Sociological Factors Behind Philippians 3:1-11 and the Conflict at Philippi," *Journal for the Study of the New Testament* 55 (1994): 97-121.
[2] Ibid.
[3] Ibid.
[4] Robert Wuthnow, *Christianity in the 21st Century: Reflections on the Challenges Ahead* (New York: Oxford University Press, 1993), 99.
[5] The reference to "a Hebrew of Hebrews" probably meant that both his parents were Israelites. Thus it is a statement about the purity of his Jewishness.
[6] All three phrases begin with the Greek preposition *kata* ("according to," "as regarding"). Probably Paul intended them to reinforce essentially one point: He, a Pharisee, lived in opposition to Jesus Christ and the gospel.
[7] Paul's reference to being "faultless" ("blameless," NASB) in this context does not indicate moral blamelessness. In the context, he was faultless or blameless as to his Judaism because he opposed the Church. The combination of references to his zeal in persecuting the Church and being declared righteous may be a reference to the Phineas episode in Numbers (Numbers 25:1-18; Psalm 106:30-31). Like Phineas, who purged Israel of unbelievers, Paul opposed those who followed Christ. But Paul's opposition was wrong.
[8] Gordon Fee, *Paul's Letter to the Philippians* (Grand Rapids, MI: Eerdmans, 1995), 316, n. 14; also Tellbe.
[9] Paul used common marketplace language, "profit" and "loss." The significance may lie in the actual Philippian situation. Since the church was attempting to ease the conflict between the gospel and the Roman "system," the economic terms are appropriate.

[10] Note the similarity between the Philippians text and Jesus' words in Matthew 16:25-26: "loses" (*zemiothe*) his life; "finds" (*euresei*) it; "gains" (*kerdese*) the whole world. See both Fee, 316, n. 11 and Moises Silva, *Philippians* (Chicago: Moody, 1988), 181.

[11] Beare, *The Epistle to the Philippians* (New York: Harper & Bros., 1969), 119, cited by David A. DeSilva in "No Confidence in the Flesh: The Meaning and Function of Philippians 3:2-21" *Trinity Journal* 15NS (1994): 27-54.

[12] DeSilva.

[13] Silva, 183.

[14] To understand more fully Paul and his teaching, we must put the Damascus Road event in better focus. Two volumes on the subject offer insight into Paul's confrontation with the risen Lord: Seyoon Kim, *The Origin of Paul's Gospel* (Grand Rapids, MI: Eerdmans, 1983) and Richard Gaffin, *Resurrection and Redemption: A Study in Paul's Soteriology* (formerly entitled *The Centrality of the Resurrection*) (Phillipsburg, NJ: Presbyterian and Reformed Publishing Co., 1987). Both books are difficult reading, Gaffin's less so. But Kim's summaries are especially helpful in understanding the apostle Paul. My own article, "Romans 1:1-5 and the Purpose of Romans: The Solution to the Two-Congregation Problem in Rome" [*Trinity Journal* (14NS, No 1): 25-40] may be a helpful resource in understanding the relationship between the gospel, the resurrection and Pauline backgrounds.

[15] Note Philippians 1:2; 2:11, 19; 3:8, 20; 4:23; and in an absolute sense see 1:14; 2:24, 29; 3:1; 4:1-2, 4-5, 10. Also see Tellbe, n. 56-58.

[16] Tellbe.

[17] The English word *and* at the head of 3:9 can and should be rendered "namely." In other words, the Greek *kai* is epexegetical. That is, 3:9 explains more fully what is meant by "gaining Christ."

[18] Fee 322, n. 35 has a good overview on this subject.

[19] For a beautiful and insightful rendering of the gospel of Jesus Christ, see Calvin Miller's *The Singer* (Downers Grove, IL: InterVarsity, 1978).

[20] Silva 189; Gerald F. Hawthorne, *Word Biblical Commentary,* Vol. 43, *Philippians* (Waco, TX: Word, 1983), 142.

[21] As in 3:8-9 (see note 17 above), the *kai* ("and") that follows the words "to know Christ" (3:10) is epexegetical. To know Christ means to know the power of His resurrection and the fellowship of His suffering.

[22] Ravi Zacharias, *Can Man Live Without God?* (Dallas, TX: Word, 1994), 53.

[23] Tellbe, n. 63.

[24] Paul's testimony parallels this thought: He was in chains (1:7-14); he faced struggle and hardship (1:12-16, 30; 3:13-14, 18; 4:1, 12-14). We will discuss this matter in our next chapter.

[25] Michael Horton, *Beyond Cultural Wars: Is America a Mission Field or a Battlefield?* (Chicago: Moody, 1994), 63.

CHAPTER 10

Spirituality on a "Higher" Standard
Philippians 3:12-21

IN HOMER'S EPIC POEM, *THE ODYSSEY,* Odysseus had to steer his ship on a hazardous course past the isle of the sirens. The singing of the sirens was irresistibly beautiful. But sailors, lured by the beautiful song, found the sirens also murderous. Once in the current of these enchanting predators, life and cargo were doomed.

Circe warned Homer's hero of the danger when he and his crew put in at Aiaia. But she also advised him how he could hear the beautiful singing and escape. As they set out, Odysseus first sealed the ears of his sailors with wax. Then, by prearrangement, they lashed him securely to the ship's main mast. Thanks to Odysseus' foresight and precautions, his ship passed safely by the island of temptation and death.

One of our most devastating "sirens" today is our culture's success mentality. It lures Christians into patterns of thought that endanger their own spiritual journey and threaten the health of the Church. Our tendency to reward success and to honor strength can cause spiritual dissatisfaction among Christians. We confuse the Christian life with American life.

Christians seem to want their Christian life to look (and feel) like American life. Alas! Herein lies the danger. The more we are lured to love our culture, the less will we be open to God's sanctifying work. The more comfortable we are with our culture, the less comfortable we will be with God. The tepid condition of the Church and countless numbers of its individual members is evidence of our choice. It is culture over sanctification.

The Philippian congregation was being lured into *"earthly"* patterns of thought (3:19) that endangered their spiritual odyssey.[1] Throughout the letter before us, Paul sets forth varying aspects of sanctification in order to restore the spiritual state of the congregation. They were to "put no confidence in the flesh" (3:3). The Philippians' spiritual life was to be measured by the person and life (and death!) of Jesus Christ (2:5-11). Precisely because they were being conformed to Christ and not to this world (1:27-30; 3:1-11), God's sanctifying work put them at tension with the world.

Now in 3:12-21, Paul plainly declares sanctification to be the process whereby the Philippians remain on spiritual course. Measuring spirituality or church ministry through *"the flesh"* is unhealthy for the individual and for the church. Rather, Paul offers a "heavenly" way of thinking about spirituality.

Spiritual Formation Is Measured in Terms of Heavenly Citizenship

Throughout 3:1-21, Paul incorporates a thematic emphasis. In 3:3-11 he cautions about putting confidence in the flesh. He encourages the Philippians to draw their meaning from Christ's death (3:10) and to strive for "the resurrection from the dead" (3:11). Now in 3:12-21, Paul continues to exhort them to consider their spiritual journey as a *"heavenly"* rather than an *"earthly"* odyssey.

Paul's threefold reference to heaven (3:14, 20-21) strongly suggests that believers' present experience is to be measured by their *future*. This reinforces thought patterns that will help them measure their spirituality from a non-earthly perspective. Richard Baxter, in his *Saints of Everlasting Rest*, appropriately said, "To be Christian, one must necessarily be heavenly." In a very real sense, that is Paul's point in 3:12-21.

Spiritual Formation Is Strengthened by Weakness

Daytime TV talk shows have taken the country by storm. A new one seems to appear every month. Typically these shows feature people whose self-image has been marred by their relationships or circumstances (for example, a teen whose mother drinks too much or a man whose father dresses like a woman). Inevitably, there is a "trained" psychologist or social worker who is "our special guest today" to render wisdom.

"You're a beautiful person," the therapist begins. "Don't gain your self-image through what others say about you. It's what's on the inside that counts, not what's on the outside."

These pop-psychologists are right—sort of. But our culture affirms just the opposite about meaningful self-image. Everywhere we turn—TV, ads, business, education—authentic meaning is experienced through success and status. Strength is prized. Weakness is a detriment.

The sad thing is that the same thought pattern exists in the Christian community. Our church growth philosophy, our ways of measuring spirituality, our leadership expectations are cut from the same piece of cloth. Success is everything. In the Christian community, too, weakness is *persona non grata.* We may *say,* "Weakness is OK." But what we affirm and honor suggests the opposite.

A Striking Confession

Repeat: *Spiritual formation is built on weakness.* Paul continually confronts our assumptions about what really matters. He begins this text with a striking confession: "Not that I have already obtained all this, or have already been made perfect" (3:12). Actually, there is no direct object for the word obtained. It is left unsaid.[2] We might assume that Paul is referring to the resurrection from the dead (3:11). This is significant in light of the false teachers who agitated the Philippian congregation.[3] The agitators, in their attempt to gain some converts at Philippi, were passing themselves off as "perfect" or "complete," having experienced already the fullness of God. They did not need to wait for the resurrection. They were already demonstrating their completeness by their fleshly accomplishments. Their present spirituality was validated by their "confidence in the flesh."

But nothing "in the flesh" or "earthly" can validate spirituality because spiritual growth and true church life are not measured by earthly success or strength. Furthermore, such a pursuit of earthly measurements for spirituality fosters, rather than diminishes, pride and status.

Paul is making an obvious contrast between himself and those who seek to validate their ministry and status by the flesh. When Paul said he was not perfect, he used a word that would have been used by those who considered themselves fully illumined and complete. Paul seems to be saying in these verses:

> *In contrast to the false teachers who seek to distract you from knowing Christ Jesus as Lord, I want you to know that even I have not come to the place where I have fully grasped*

or comprehended knowing Christ. I must await the final resurrection in order to come to this full knowledge of Him. (Author's paraphrase)

Paul redirects the focus of the Philippians' spiritual and church life by admitting he has not obtained the resurrection. The resurrection would end his journey of knowing Christ.[4] Paul humbly concedes that he has not already been made perfect (3:12). [5] Humility can only be reached and secured when the members of a congregation stop putting confidence "in the flesh" and realize they are yet incomplete in their knowledge of Christ.

An admission of weakness and incompleteness (contrary to our culture) keeps us from validating our spirituality "by the flesh." This admission of incompleteness and weakness produces genuine humility (2:3-4, 6-8; 2 Corinthians 13:9). Paul is not simply wasting his ink by admitting his weakness. He is not beating his chest in altruistic contrition. Not at all! This position of weakness means that Paul must do something.

Allow Christ to Grasp You

Since Paul has yet to experience knowing Christ fully, he says, "I press on to take hold of that for which Christ Jesus took hold of me" (Philippians 3:12). He has not arrived at his goal, so he commits himself to pursue it with all his might. This is the pattern of thought that will produce unity and joyous perseverance within the Christian worshiping community. Paul draws from hunting imagery, where the hunters chase and hunt down their prey.[6] The impression is one of movement. The pursuer is focused on what matters most: in this case, knowing Christ.

God's prior action of "apprehending" Paul is the motivating factor that gives both the heavenly resource for accomplishing the goal (1:6; 2:12-13) and explains what "prey" we are to pursue. When Paul says, "Christ Jesus took hold of me," he likely refers to his experience on the Damascus Road (Acts 9:3-6; 22:6-10; 26:12-18). That is significant to defining the words *knowing Christ Jesus as Lord.*

We hear Christians say, "I want to know Christ," or, "I want to know God." I have come to the place where I invariably respond with a question: "What does 'knowing' Christ (or God) mean to you?" Of course, the answers vary. But they usually lack any substantial element of action. One would get the impression that knowing Christ is either a cognitive pursuit or a privatized adventure involving how the person feels about his or her relationship to God.

Indeed, on the Damascus Road, Paul was "saved"—born again—when he was apprehended by Jesus. But we must think about this a bit more holistically. When Paul was confronted by Jesus, he was called to a Person *and* to a task (cf. Galatians 1:15-16). Pressing on in the pursuit of knowing Christ means, then, to surrender to Him as Lord (Philippians 3:8) *and* to participate in the task of proclaiming the good news concerning Him.

In Philippians 2:2, Paul calls the congregation at Philippi to *act*—literally, to *think one way.* They were not to be selfish. They were to be humble. Here, Paul calls upon them to pursue the one main thing of knowing Christ. No doubt the apostle was reminding them of his earlier call to them for humble service toward others. Now he offers some principles for working toward humility.

Paul moves from his hunting imagery to strike the portrait of a runner. "Forgetting what is behind and straining toward what is ahead," says (3:13). The words indicate *how*[7] Paul can win the race, the pursuit of knowing Christ and the power of His resurrection. The humble servant of God pictures himself as a runner, straining toward the finish line.

His body is bent over. His head stretches out to cross the tape. He is undistracted by the other runners. He is "paying no attention to what is behind and straining toward what is ahead."[8]

Throwing Javelins

At Dublin (New Hampshire) High School, my favorite teacher was John White. Besides science, he taught me how to ski jump, cross-country ski and mountain climb. He helped me to become a fairly good soccer player (varsity!), and he encouraged me to join the track team. I'm still not tall, but in high school I was extremely short (five feet, zero inches, to be exact). I was also a bit (shall we say) pleasantly plump. So what does a short, overweight guy do on a track team? What John White did, of course!

When he was in high school, Mr. White threw the javelin. I am sure it was quite comical the first time my teammates saw me throwing the javelin. My shortness was definitely a problem. Not only did my arms inhibit a long, arching throw, but when I leaned back to throw it, the other end of the javelin stuck in the ground! With Mr. White's help, however, I became our team's best javelin thrower.

The first track meet was nerve-racking, to say the least. When we gave our names to the referees, I signed up to throw last for my team. Normally, a team's best goes last. The other team all laughed and made snide comments when they saw our team's "best." And when I saw their best, I died. Six feet, four inches—and still growing!

My first throw was so short I wanted to leave right then. My second throw was out of bounds. To make matters worse, I twisted my ankle. Why even try the third throw?

My weakness was only magnified as I compared myself with those throwing on the other team. But that all disappeared when John White came to watch my final attempt. To me, his presence was the only thing that mattered.

Did he care that I won? Not really. He knew my limitations. But, nonetheless, I would do my best.

And do my best I did—my longest throw ever! (And, if you must know, I placed first. Although the other team's "best" out threw me, *he was distracted* by my last throw and his last did not break ground. There's a lesson there, too, I am sure!)

Our spiritual journey is very similar to my javelin-throwing experience. We have every weakness imaginable. That is why we must continually forget (note the present tense) what is in the past. Paul had to forget his status as a blameless Law-keeper. He had to forget the years he persecuted the Church and blasphemed the name of Jesus.[9] He had to forget the attacks of his accusers and the opposition.

You know what *you* must forget.

Our spiritual odyssey to know Christ will be a continuous, deliberate admission of our weakness. *We cannot count on how well we did spiritually in the past. Nor how poorly.* Making judgments based on past failures or successes or on how others are doing will hinder our present spiritual growth.

Earthly accomplishments (and failures) can distract us from future spiritual growth. We need to join Paul in his forward, heavenward race. He says, "I press on toward the goal to win the prize for which God has called me heavenward in Christ Jesus " (3:14). Paul no longer judges his life and ministry by earthly standards. These would distract him from his goal of knowing Christ Jesus.

Spiritual Formation Is Molded by Humility, Not by Accomplishment or Status

Over the years I have had the privilege of mentoring future church leaders. At times, the powers-that-be would gather us mentors for seminars. At one such seminar, I encountered a rather cavalier attitude both among my fellow mentors and on the part of those conducting the seminar. We were given a "problem" scenario that we might encounter when working with an intern. It was this:

> *The intern is not fulfilling the agreed-upon contract for activities and work. He/she has been talked to about this but he/she continues to set aside the prearranged agreement in favor of other activities he/she deems more important. What should the mentor do?*

The mentors had some suggestions. One mentor thought the intern should be confronted about the problem. Another favored involving the church elders.

"Perhaps I, the mentor, and the church board ought to reevaluate the contract," I suggested. "We need to reevaluate the student's abilities and the church's present needs. Perhaps the intern is right. Perhaps the church's needs have changed, or we have identified the wrong needs for the intern to meet."

Wrong answer! That was not what the leaders of the seminar wanted. Without question, the-intern-is-the-problem was the implication.

I might have dismissed the apparent attitude as an aberration had it not cropped up again later in the seminar. Of course, interns need to be submissive. They need to respect the authority of the pastor and the church board. But what I witnessed was an attitude that interns could not possibly be right and mentors could not possibly be wrong—period!

Paul rather clearly identifies and involves Church leadership in his effort to restore the Church's unity and persevering joy (3:15). Although *everyone* should apply the principles, Church leaders are responsible for setting the pace. They are to lead in humility as servants (cf. 1:1).

Someone once said, "As the leadership goes, so goes the Church." It is so.

"If on Some Point You Think Differently . . ."

There is something both sarcastic and poignant about Paul's words, "All of us who are mature" (3:15). The English word *mature* masks Paul's repetition of the *teleios* wordplay throughout these verses (3:12ff.). There is a dual allusion here. On the one hand, his letter is intended for the "overseers and deacons" of the church (1:1)—the church leadership. On the other, he seems to be inferring that at least some of these very leaders need God to clarify their thinking. Were some of the leaders guilty of "fleshly" thinking about true spirituality?

Changing the Philippians' pattern of thinking has been a main concern for Paul throughout the letter. The NIV does not reflect well this aspect in 3:15.

Paul uses the demonstrative pronoun *touto* (rendered "this" by the NIV translators) with the verb "to think." It is similar to his exhortation to "think the mind of Christ" (2:5). He seems to be saying, "Think the way in which I have indicated." In other words, the church leaders should "put no confidence in the flesh" (3:3ff.). They should not consider themselves to have already obtained the full *teleios* that will only come in the following life. Full knowledge of Christ is a prize yet future, and we "press on toward the goal to win the prize for which God has called [us] heavenward in Christ Jesus" (3:14).[10]

The Philippians are to share Paul's frame of mind. They are to apply the admission of weakness (3:12-13) to their spiritual growth.

Think about it for a moment. What kinds of gauges do we use to measure our spiritual growth? What models do we emulate? What do we affirm as spiritual? Whom do we honor and consider spiritual? The answers to those questions will demonstrate how we define spirituality, church growth and our own Christian identity.

Paul Admits His Weaknesses

It is important to note that when Paul defends his ministry—his own leadership—he draws not upon his strengths but his weaknesses. He writes to the Corinthians:

> *In Damascus the governor under King Aretas had the city of the Damascenes guarded in order to arrest me. But I was lowered in a basket from a window in the wall and slipped through his hands.* (2 Corinthians 11:32-33)

Paul ran! Some "super-apostle" he was! In fact, this fellow would rather boast in his weaknesses:

> *I will boast all the more gladly about my weaknesses, so that Christ's power may rest on me. That is why, for Christ's sake, I delight in weakness, in insults, in hardships, in persecutions, in difficulties. For when I am weak, then I am strong.* (2 Corinthians 12:9-10)

We can only surmise what contributed to Paul's weakness. Before this admission, he said, "There was given me a thorn in my flesh" (2 Corinthians 12:7). This thorn (*skolops*) was more like a spear than a sliver embedded in a finger. Paul Bubna comments, "It is safe to say it [was] a fairly noticeable sort of thing."[11]

The apostle's appearance was uncomplimentary and his preaching was unimpressive (10:10; 11:6). His poor eyesight left him dependent on others. Whatever his thorn, it was ever present to remind him that God's "grace is sufficient" and God's "power is made perfect in weakness" (12:9).

Paul knew full well that ministry which flows from strength and success can deteriorate into human-centered activities. People become the focus and God's power and honor are effectively diminished.

I overheard the pastor of a substantial church remark, "I don't give my interns a lot of preaching time because there are high-powered executives in the congregation, and they expect quality preaching." Under the pressure of the market orientation advocated by the church-growth people, that comment was understandable. Yet it also points up the "fleshly" levels to which we have succumbed in order to "grow."

The problem lies not in the "high-powered" people but in the church leadership. We are not teaching our lay people well. We can demonstrate the American model of success and strength in our leadership if we choose. But we will fashion our churches after the image of our culture rather than after Christ.

Paul is hopeful that the leadership will repent. Realistically, however, he expected some continued opposition. (After all, what leader likes to admit weakness!) So he says, "And if on some point you think differently, that too God will make clear to you" (Philippians 3:15). The apostle knew that it would take a combination of his own persuasion (the letter he was writing) and God's continued work in the hearts and minds of the leaders. Silva suggests Paul is saying, "But if there continue to be some conflicts among you, I trust that God will soon bring unanimity in your midst."[12]

Returning to the abcs of Spiritual Growth
In order to restore a proper perspective for measuring (and pursuing) joyous spirituality, Paul returns to the ABCs of the faith. He instructs the Philippians, "Only let us live up to what we have already attained" (3:16). Paul uses the word *stoichein,* from which we get such concepts as "step-by-step"

or "saying our ABCs." Often the word is translated "live up to" or "live in conformity with." To the Galatians Paul wrote, "Since we live by the Spirit, let us keep in step [*stoichomen*] with the Spirit" (Galatians 5:25). In other words, Paul is asking all to bring their lives into line with a previously set standard.

This standard is the salvation they have already attained through the death of Christ on the cross. They were saved by God's power, not by their human prowess. It was the "foolishness" of God (1 Corinthians 1:18-31), not the wisdom of humankind, that saved them. Paul warned the Colossians: "See to it that no one takes you captive through hollow and deceptive philosophy, which depends on human tradition and the basic principles [*stoicheia*] of this world rather than on Christ" (2:8). Thus Jesus through His death is not only the avenue of our salvation, but He is the measure of our spiritual development and of our church ministry (Philippians 2:5-11).

Let's admit it. We North Americans do not approach ministry through weakness but through the prevailing mentality of managerial strength. I was saddened recently when I read a sociologist's comment on modern Church leadership. "When I meet a Hindu leader," the sociologist said, "I meet a holy man. When I meet a [Christian] church leader, I meet a manager." This success-strength mentality of present Church leadership trickles down to the rank-and-file. It forms in them patterns of thought and habits that affirm attitudes counter to biblical models of ministry and spirituality. The result? Continued damage to the health of the Church.

Our Spiritual Formation Is Patterned after Another World
November 22, 1963, is a date etched into the American psyche. It was on that date that United States President John Fitzgerald Kennedy was assassinated in Dallas, Texas. It

just so happened that two other famous people died that same day within hours of one another: C.S. Lewis, Christian writer and apologist, and Aldous Huxley, novelist and critic.

In his book *Between Heaven and Hell* Peter Kreeft presents a fictitious, after-death conversation between these three men in what Kreeft terms "that other world."[13] Before Huxley appears, Kreeft has Lewis and Kennedy talking. At one point the conversation turns toward religion.

> "I did not really have time for religion,"
> Kennedy confesses to Lewis. "I had to live in
> one world at a time—one at a time."
> Lewis' eyes pan the "room" where the two of
> them are waiting. "Obviously, Mr. President,"
> Lewis replies, "it is two worlds at a time."

Therein is the difficulty. The Christian lives in two worlds at the same time. But our tendency is to live now "according to this world" and let the eternal world wait. Our preference is for one world at a time. Our temptation is to pattern our lives after the "flesh" because that makes us more comfortable with the one world that we can touch, taste and handle. It is "this world" that gives us outward affirmation for measuring spirituality and church ministry. Paul, however, exhorts us, "Join with others in following my example...Take note of those who live according to the pattern we gave you" (3:17).

But not all the misdirected leaders were within the Philippian church. As I mentioned earlier, the Egnatian Way, the main overland route between the East and Rome, ran through Philippi. Doubtless the Philippian Christians frequently extended hospitality to itinerant preachers traveling in the region.[14] Paul has already offered criteria that would determine who was honorable and deserving of their welcome (2:19-30).

The Philippians as well as Paul faced some measure of tension with Rome (3:1-11). Paul has already referred to his personal tension with Rome. (He is under Roman arrest!) So he sees his own struggles as not dissimilar to those of his readers. In fact, he has already told them so: "You are going through the same struggle you saw I had, and now hear that I still have" (1:30).

Thus Paul's own testimony and experience (3:4-14) *is* the way to maintain one's spiritual growth and to restore the church's spiritual health.[15]

The command to "take note" (*skopeite*) of those who live according to his example (3:17) means "keep your eye on," "observe carefully." Paul must have chosen the word deliberately to recall his pursuit of the goal, the *skopos* of the heavenward call of God (see 3:14).[16] "Model yourselves," Paul is saying, "after those whose own patterns of thought and behavior are consistent with the gospel and Christ Jesus."

Spiritually Dangerous Formation

There were those who patterned their Christianity after what was contrary to the cross of Christ. As a result, the life of the church in Philippi was at stake and the gospel itself was at risk. Paul's emotions were running high. "I have often told you before," he says, "and now say again even with tears, many live as enemies of the cross of Christ" (3:18).

It is instructive that Paul said "enemies of *the cross* of Christ" rather than simply "enemies of Christ." In this context the difference is significant. The cross reveals not only our weakness but God's *method* for evaluating everything (2 Corinthians 5:16-21; Philippians 2:6-11). The cross is God's utter contradiction to human wisdom and power. We, too, can become enemies of the cross when our method for evaluating spiritual growth (whether personal growth or church growth) is patterned after the "success and strength" models of our American culture.

The "end" (3:19, NASB) of those who prize success and strength will be their own destruction. Here Paul uses a wordplay to underscore the false confidence that the false teachers had about their false perfection (*teleioi,* 3:12, 15). Since they seek to demonstrate their spiritual state in terms of "fleshly" measurements, they later will discover their real "destiny [*telos*] is destruction."

Likewise, when Paul comments about these enemies by saying "their god is their stomach," he is indicating that their fleshly impulses drive their spiritual mentality. It is not so much immorality at issue or a form of antinomianism. Rather, these enemy leaders sought to validate their spiritual authority and ministry in terms of their fleshly desires. In Romans 16:17-18, Paul refers to certain ones as servants "not [of] our Lord Christ, but [of] their own appetites."[17] The final judgment will turn their present glory into their eternal shame. Those who seek to validate their spiritual growth or success in Christian ministry by the flesh demonstrate that "[t]heir mind is on earthly things" (Philippians 3:19).

This brings us full circle. All the way through this letter, Paul has been attempting to redirect the Philippians' thinking. Those who have "confidence in the flesh" are not patterning their Christian lives, their ministries, their church congregations after the gospel. Neither are they conforming their lives after the One who "made himself nothing" and "humbled himself" (2:7-8). Instead, they have their own self-interests in mind—no matter how noble their ideas appear or how seemingly good their intentions are.

Our American culture confers award, merit and prestige on those who demonstrate success and strength. But in the end, any spiritual formation that puts "confidence in the flesh" is dangerous, both for the individual and the Church.

Our Heavenly Citizenship

Our patterns of thought and behavior are to stem not from our earthly existence but from our heavenly citizenship. "Our citizenship is in heaven," Paul tells the Philippians (3:20).[18] It was essentially the same word he gave to the believers at Ephesus (Ephesians 1:3, 20; 2:6; 3:10; 6:12). But in Philippi the reference took on special significance because of the city's special loyalty to Rome and Caesar. Those who now named Jesus, rather than Caesar, as Lord were in immediate tension with Rome. Their faith in Christ had put their Roman citizenship in question. But Paul is telling them their identity must stem not from Rome or from the local culture but from heaven.

The Greek word for citizenship is *politeuma*. Its first meaning is a commonwealth or state. But it can also mean a colony of foreigners who "in the environment of their present residence outside their native country" live according to the laws and principles of, not the land they live in, but of their native home.[19] In this context, Paul is saying the Philippians' spirituality (that is, the measure for spiritual and church growth) must be according to the principles of their new homeland—heaven (Philippians 1:26-3:21).

Paul brings this text—and, really, his whole discussion of sanctification since 1:26—to its climax with an emphasis of this point. The object of our devotion is not heaven itself but the Savior who will come from heaven (not Rome!), the Lord Jesus Christ. This Lord is the one who has "everything under his control" (3:21). The Christian community in Philippi might be in tension with the surrounding culture. But the Object of their faith, Jesus Christ the Lord, not the flesh and not the culture, is to be their confidence for all of life.

It is this Lord who "will transform [their] lowly bodies so that they will be like his glorious body" (3:21). The NIV rendering, "lowly bodies," masks the impact of

Paul's statement. More literally it should read "the body of our humiliation" (*tapeivoseos*).[20] This state of humiliation should remind all that they cannot count on the flesh for validation. These human bodies will continue to be reminders of humanity's fallenness, weakness, selfishness. This side of heaven, our lives will be marked by "frailty, suffering, sorrow, vanity, death and corruption."[21]

Echoing his earlier confession of weakness, the apostle concludes that our bodies—the point of contact between ourselves and our world—will keep us humble. But it will be our Lord Jesus Christ who will transform the bodies of our humiliation into bodies like His own. When He comes from heaven at the *eschaton* (the end of time), Jesus' body will be incorruptible and glorious (1 Corinthians 15:20-58; 2 Corinthians 4:16-5:10; 1 John 3:1-4).

Our Heavenly Citizenship Lifts Us above Our Dying Culture

We must remember that Paul's testimony throughout 3:1-21 was offered to enhance the Church's health. Paul gave it not simply to model successful Christian living. We can turn the deeper Christian life into another "law" if we enter it for the wrong reasons. It will simply be another earthly confidence if we enter it to validate our feelings about our relationship with God. The deeper life in Christ is not something for just our private sphere. For it truly to be a Spirit experience, it must put us in a place to benefit the Church. It must put us where we can participate in the gospel.

When we use our culture's measurements for success, our sanctification takes on elements destructive to personal spirituality and Church life. Paul harnesses his whole range of theology and experience with Christ to set forth a model of sanctification for the Church. We must be alert for teachings (whether from Christians or secular society) that affirm our culture's expectations rather than the gospel's. That is Paul's point!

Calvary Church pastor Ed Dobson remarks:

> I think we are losing the culture war, not in the public arena, but *within the Church.* Until we renew what it means to be a Christian *in the Church,* we won't have credibility to speak to the world (my emphasis).[22]

Certainly our message needs to be relevant to the times. But we do not necessarily achieve relevancy by imitating our culture. As someone once remarked, the Church must raise itself above the fate of a dying culture if it is not to share that fate.

In order to seize our own moment in time, we must be seized by Jesus Christ. In his book *The Evangelical Forfeit* John Seel writes:

> We must hold dear the first things of the gospel of Jesus Christ. If we hold fast to the gospel of salvation, if we maintain our hope of glory and if we are obedient to his call of radical discipleship in this age, God may bring revival and reformation to our land, our culture and his church.[23]

Endnotes

[1] I purposely chose the phrase "patterns of thought" because it best fits Paul's thinking throughout Philippians. It is hard to separate thinking and behavior. But how we experience life molds our thinking and reinforces thought patterns that can be spiritually healthy or spiritually devastating. This can be seen in the church-growth philosophy and in material on "successful" spiritual living. This creates thought patterns that conform us to our culture and harm both our spirituality

and church life.

[2] Many ambiguities exist in the New Testament for one of two reasons. First, New Testament writers often assumed certain knowledge and understanding by the recipients. It is like listening to one side of a telephone conversation. We hear what is clear and do our best to discover the "other side of the conversation," the original situation or occasion for the call. Second, the Greek language provided for many elliptical expressions (things understood and therefore omitted). In the case of 3:12-13, refer to both my brief description of the letter's occasion (see Introduction) and my commentary in chapter 9. For discussions of the ambiguous nature of 3:12-13, consult the three major commentaries that I have been referring to throughout my own exegesis: Gerald F. Hawthorne, *Word Biblical Commentary,* Vol. 43, *Philippians* (Waco, TX: Word, 1983); Gordon Fee, *Paul's Letter to the Philippians* (Grand Rapids, MI: Eerdmans, 1995); Moises Silva, *Philippians* (Chicago, IL: Moody, 1988).

[3] Various commentators find at least three groups opposing Paul in Philippi: (1) false preachers (see 1:12ff), (2) Judaizing missionaries (see 3:2) and (3) Gnostic teachers (see 3:12ff). These commentators may be right. But perhaps it is best to regard Paul's opponents in Philippi as coming from the same mold as those in Rome. The "mirror reading" of the letter to the Philippians (see my chapter 9) seems to suggest that Paul is contrasting his teaching with the teaching of Judaizers who believed they had arrived at perfection or full illumination (compare the terminology Paul uses in 3:12). For further discussion of Paul's opposition, see also the introductions in Hawthorne, Silva and Fee.

[4] The word *obtained* has a wide range of meanings, including "apprehension" or "comprehending something." John says the Jews did not "understand" the coming of Jesus (John 1:5). Peter came to "realize" that God was welcoming Gentiles into the Church (Acts 10:34). And Paul prayed that

the Ephesians would "grasp" the fullness of God in Christ (Ephesians 3:18; Ephesians 3:8, 10). See Hawthorne, 150-151; Fee, 343; contra Silva, 199-200.

[5] The use of *perfect* is twofold. First, this word can carry a broad range of meaning: "complete," "perfect," "mature." Some commentators also note that a cognitive aspect is within the range of meaning as well. For example, Paul uses *teleoio* to refer to mature thinking (1 Corinthians 14:20). Given the "knowing" context of Philippians 3, this understanding seems reasonable in 3:12-15.

[6] Hawthorne, 152.

[7] Verse 13 is composed of "circumstantial" participles, explaining how Paul determined to "run the race." See Hawthorne, 153.

[8] Fee, 347.

[9] Paul's use of the word *dioko* ("pursue") is a wordplay on his past persecution of the Church. *Dioko* is the word often used to indicate persecution. Paul is saying: "I once *pursued* the church by persecuting it. In this I was the worst of sinners. But now I have been forgiven and I *pursue* knowing the Lord of the Church with all my might."

[10] Fee, 356.

[11] Paul F. Bubna, *Second Corinthians: Ministry: God at Work in Me for the Good of Others* (*Second Corinthians*) (Camp Hill, PA: Christian Publications, 1993), 168.

[12] Silva, 206.

[13] Peter Kreeft, *Between Heaven and Hell* (Downers Grove, IL: InterVarsity, 1982), 13-14.

[14] Fee, 366.

[15] Additional references where Paul exhorts others to imitate him: 1 Thessalonians 1:6, 2:14; 2 Thessalonians 3:7, 9; 1 Corinthians 4:16; 11:1 (Hebrews 6:12; 13:7; 3 John 11).

[16] Silva, 208. Possibly Paul chose the word *skopeite* because it recalled for him his reference in his Corinthian letter to the *skolops* ("thorn") that God had used to "strengthen" him.

[17] Silva, 208-210.

[18] Verses 18-19 and 20-21 function as the reason the Philippians were to pattern their lives after Paul (3:17). It is as though Paul was saying: "You are to define your Christian existence and measure your spirituality by the gospel. Even though you find yourselves in conflict with the culture around you, do not seek to define your Christian life by means of society's expectations and assumptions about 'meaningfulness' and 'fulfillment.' Although these will make you *feel* more comfortable with living in the world, they will put you at odds with the gospel and with Jesus Christ Himself. Therefore, since you, like me, are in conflict with the culture, define yourselves and your spirituality through knowing Christ. Make this your total commitment. Why? Because, first, those who put confidence in the flesh are enemies of the cross of Christ (3:18-19). And, second, because you are defined by your heavenly existence (3:20-21)."

[19] W.M. Smith, "Heaven," *Zondervan Pictorial Encyclopedia of the Bible,* Vol. 3, ed. Merrill C. Tenney (Grand Rapids, MI: Zondervan, 1975), 60-64.

[20] Note that Paul uses the same word in 2:8 to describe Jesus: "being found in appearance as a man, he humbled [*etapeinosen*] himself / and became obedient to death— even death on a cross!"

[21] Hawthorne, 172.

[22] John Seel, *The Evangelical Forfeit: Can We Recover?* (Grand Rapids, MI: Baker, 1993), 114.

[23] Ibid., 116.

CHAPTER 11

All Sail and No Anchor: The Cost of Freedom
Philippians 4:1-9

I LOVE BOATS, ESPECIALLY SAILBOATS. When I was a boy, I spent many Saturday afternoons sailing on my dad's sloop in Long Island Sound. Even as a kid, I sensed the freedom when the winds filled the sails and the boat cut its way through the water. I loved it!

One of the hallmarks of North American life is our sense of freedom. But freedom is not without cost. We love our freedom—but what about the price? We are too uncritical of the freedoms we enjoy. We regard them as neutral. We accept them as entitlements. Someone once remarked about the United States: "We are all sail and no anchor."

Freedom enhances individualism. At the same time, it diminishes community. Therein lies its price. A community cannot survive without some deferment of individual freedom. Today, however, in North America, nothing is secure. Everything from toys to styles to relationships is thrown to the winds of freedom.

The Church Has Not Escaped the Freedom Syndrome

Even the Church can be all sail and anchorless. Often our style of worship, our behavior as Christians, even what is proclaimed from our pulpits must defer to personal freedom. American freedom has so conditioned Christian thinking and Christian habits that even the Church—*your* church—is threatened. We make the gospel appealing to non-Christians by showing how Jesus *frees* them. We appeal to their "need" for fulfillment and self-identity. If they sign on and we ask them to serve their church, they exercise their entitlement to freedom and decline. Others exercise their freedom by "church-shopping," looking for the church that caters most nearly to their individual preferences.

In America we have stood the Christian life on its head. Self-interest has risen to replace self-sacrifice. Self-expression has replaced dying to self. The letter to the Philippians reverses this cultural flow. The apostle's message confronts our privatized faith square on. It seeks to restore the Christian's proper attitude toward his or her church.

Paul began his letter by drawing the Philippians' attention to the relationship between the Church and the work of the gospel (1:3-30). Then he called upon his readers to defer self-interests for the sake of the Church—their own local church! (2:1-30). Then he asked the Philippians to recommit themselves to the essentials of the faith, namely, the death and resurrection of Jesus Christ (3:1-21). All of this was to inspire unity, harmony, and mutual concern within the whole congregation for the sake of the gospel.

Paul did not appeal to the "freedom" his readers had in Christ.[1] Rather, he appealed with concrete solutions that flowed from God's work in the Church (1:6; 2:12-13) and the "work of Jesus Christ" (1:22; 3:1-21).

Now, in the remaining two texts, 4:1-9 and 4:10-20, we will note how Paul applied his gospel to the church at Philippi. This *paraenesis* or application section, 4:1-20, is not an arbitrary set of commands detached from his discussion until now. His emphasis on sanctification (1:27-3:21) was to inspire certain character traits that would enhance unity and help the whole congregation to "[contend] as one man for the faith of the gospel" (1:27; cf. 4:3). Sanctification indeed leads to practical holiness. But practical holiness leads not just to personal piety (that is, our contemporary, privatized faith), but also to personal responsibility for our local churches.

Character Traits That Bring Unity

Paul is about to bring his exhortation to its climax.[2] The beginning of the application section functions as a link to his previous exhortations. Paul has called upon the Church members to walk as worthy citizens (*politeuesthe*, 1:27a; cf. 3:20) of the gospel of Christ. They are to stand (*stekete*, 1:27b; cf. 4:1), striving together (*synathountes*, 1:27c; cf. 4:3) for the sake of the gospel. Now, in 4:1ff, Paul explains the manner (*outos*) by which they are to stand together. He says, "[This] is how you should stand firm in the Lord, dear friends!"

Paul returns to his very evident affection for these his children in the Lord. He had told them earlier, "I long for all of you with the affection of Christ Jesus" (1:8). He said, "I have you in my heart" (1:7). Now he adds that some of these "have contended at my side in the cause of the gospel" (4:3).

The apostle has just referred to the Philippian congregation as his "joy and crown" (4:1). This reference to a crown (*stephanos*) draws on his previous "runner" imagery (3:14). But more than that, it also implies that the Philippian Christians will be his reward when his Lord returns to this earth. As Paul remarked to the Thessalonians: "What is our hope, our joy, or the crown [*stephanos*] in which we will glory in the presence of our Lord Jesus when he comes? Is it not you? ... You are our glory and joy"

(1 Thessalonians 2:19-20). Paul's commitment to "stand firm" had resulted in a crown—namely, the people he had won to the Lord. In this instance, the Philippian converts *were* his crown.

In the context of Philippi and the Philippian correspondence, this is a significant admission for Paul. He had put his own self-interests aside in order to bring the gospel to Philippi. His preaching there had put him in conflict with Roman society. He and Silas had been beaten mercilessly and jailed (Acts 16:11-30). He and Silas had deferred their freedom for another reward: those who would be converted in Philippi through the good news Paul and Silas proclaimed. The Philippians needed—and we today need—to develop similar character traits. God looks for local communities of faith that will strive together for the sake of the gospel.

Work Unitedly for the Cause of the Gospel
Many contemporary church-growth strategies encourage congregations to settle on a potential target group: young marrieds, empty-nesters, early retirees, for example. In theory this allows the church to develop as a homogeneous group. Adherents share common experiences. They feel comfortable with each other. They "belong."

The idea seems reasonable enough. But it is not necessarily appropriate for the gospel. Such an approach to church growth focuses on social, economic, racial, educational relationships. In other words, it focuses on self-interests, on elements of our cultural life. That turns Paul's exhortation in 3:1-11 upside down. Instead, we should be focused on Jesus Christ. Our identity, our bond of unity, is *in Him,* not in our culture. It is spiritual, not material and earthly (Galatians 3; Ephesians 4:3-16; Colossians 2:8; 3:1-4; Romans 6:1-14). The Church is to be comprised of all people, from all walks of life. Local churches are not Christian forums or caucuses. Each one is to be a reflection of the unlikely but remarkable joining of diverse people. Cultural and social differences are bridged by Christ's redeeming love. The goal is to work together "in the cause of the gospel" (4:3).

Earle Palmer, referring to something C.S. Lewis once said, observed,

> Mutuality is the key to the oneness of the tennis club or the trade union, but not [of] Christians. We are brought together because of Christ's invitation, and the people He puts us alongside...may well be "that very selection of neighbors we have been avoiding all week."[3]

Paul next has some words of exhortation for two women whose apparent *dis*agreement was deprecating the gospel. He writes: "I plead with Euodia and I plead with Syntyche to agree with each other in the Lord" (4:2). With little doubt, these two women were among the leaders in the Philippian congregation (1:1 and 3:15). Certainly they were not from the Judaizing agitators or from Paul's opposition.[4] Paul singles out the two women precisely because they were his coworkers. "[They] have contended at my side in the cause of the gospel," he recalls (4:3). Whatever the issue of disagreement between the two, it fed disunity within the ranks.

"Think the Same Things in the Lord"
Paul pleads with these two women "to agree with each other." The Greek wording behind this phrase is similar to other "thinking" texts in Philippians (1:7, 27; 2:2, 5; 3:15, 19; 4:2, 10). Literally, Paul asked them to "think the same things [*to auto phronein*] in the Lord."

Paul has been commenting about "enemies of the

cross of Christ" whose "mind is on earthly things" (3:18-19). We may assume, therefore, that these two women were provoking conflict in line with the false teaching in Philippi. Whether through the false missionaries or the cultural conflicts (cf. 3:1-11), these women displayed wrong thinking. The result was further disunity or rivalry. Paul implores them to repent. He begs them to return to right thinking that produces faithful obedience to Christ Jesus.

The Philippians were "put[ting] confidence in the flesh." That was the general nature of the problem. Outside of this, we do not know the specifics. We hold that Paul wrote under the inspiration of the Holy Spirit. The fact that Paul is not specific permits us to apply his caution and exhortation more generally. *All* Christians who cause conflict in the Church need to do some self-evaluating. Are they, in some way, "put[ting] confidence in the flesh"?

Although Paul was "case specific" in his application, the enduring principle that applies to every generation of believers comes through his emphasis on teamwork. "Yes, and I ask you, loyal yokefellow, help these women who have contended at my side in the cause of the gospel, along with Clement and the rest of my fellow workers, whose names are in the book of life" (4:3).

We cannot identify the "loyal yokefellow" whom Paul addresses. (Note that the NIV translators suggest the word *yokefellow* may be a man's name—Syzygus.) What *does* seem apparent is that Paul is seeking to create a sense of teamwork. Paul does not call on the two women to patch up their differences by themselves. He elicits another's help. In his inspired application of truth, Paul is emphasizing the corporate responsibility of the church to pull together and to fulfill its mission.[5] That makes sense. Repeatedly, he has expressed concern for the church's health. He has sought to involve the whole body in the healing process. He continues to emphasize that point.

"Suspended in Glorious, but Terrifying, Isolation"?

The authors of the book *Habits of the Heart* make an astute observation: "American cultural traditions define personality, achievement and the purpose of human life in ways that leave the individual suspended in glorious, but terrifying, isolation."[6] Not so those contending for the gospel. They—we—do not persevere in isolation. The character of the Church is built on teamwork (1:27; 2:12-14; 1 Corinthians 12-14; Romans 12; Ephesians 4:1-16). The Church is a community. This is crucial to the Church's health and the increase of God's kingdom.

We confront an alarming phenomenon in the United States—and possibly Canada, too. Christians switch churches as readily as they do breakfast cereals or laundry detergent. In our competitive society of multiple choices, responsibility for and to a local church has fast eroded. Christians put their individualism above the well-being of their church (Philippians 2:1-4, 5-8, 12-15, 19-30).

In *The Screwtape Letters,* C.S. Lewis has Screwtape writing to Wormwood, the underling-in-training:

> Surely you know that if a man can't be cured
> of churchgoing, the next best thing is to send
> him all over the neighborhood looking for
> the church that "suits" him until he becomes
> a taster or connoisseur of churches.[7]

Lewis understood well the attitudes that are bred in an atmosphere of individualism. He puts these final words in the mouth of Screwtape: "The search for the 'suitable' church makes the man a critic where the Enemy [God] wants him to be a pupil!"

When everyone is a critic, it is hard to develop a mind of humility.

Paul's solution for dissension in the ranks runs

counter to our culture of individualism and self-expression. Despite hurt feelings and agitation caused by some individuals, Christians are to pull together as an expression of God's grace in Christ Jesus. Those who "think differently" (3:15) from the majority are nevertheless to work together for harmony. Let everyone be responsible for mending the rifts. Let each member help forge an uncompromising alliance for the sake of the gospel. All are to work together. And that means working together on the unpleasant task of working out the problems.

Paul's reference to "the book of life" (4:3) is also significant.[8] Again and again, he has called the church to look to its heavenly future or to live in the light of that future (1:6, 10, 21-23; 2:11, 16; 3:12-14, 20-21; 4:1, 5). Similarly, he has reminded the Philippians that their true identity is found not in the flesh but in their heavenly position in Christ Jesus. The records that count are not at city hall in Philippi. They are in the heavenly book of life— including the names Euodia and Syntyche.

The Community of Faith Must Strive for Attitudes That Bind It Together

E.M. Bounds wrote: "People are God's method. The church is looking for better methods; God is looking for better people."[9] The Church today is a far cry from this clarion call for godly people. We have turned everything on its head. By establishing church growth and church life on the basis of self-interest, churches become more concerned about methodology than godliness. This concentration on methodology reinforces our privatized faith and increases the casualties of our individualism.

The church at Philippi faced both internal and external strife. Those pressures fed attitudes and prompted actions that caused disunity. Disunity, in turn, put the gospel at risk. In order for the church to stand and to contend for the cause of the gospel, the members needed a frame of mind that would bind them together as one. In these verses Paul calls for attitudes and actions that will counter the problems facing the congregation.

Rejoice in the Essentials.

Joy heads the list. Joy will help to bring harmony to the congregation. It will restore the church's vitality. "Rejoice in the Lord always. I will say it again: Rejoice!" (4:4). Paul's use of "joy" words in this letter is split between expressions of his own joy and exhortations to the Philippians to have joy. His prayers on behalf of the Philippians were offered in joy (1:4). His joy amid trying circumstances was a model for the Philippians to imitate (1:18, 30; 2:17; 3:17; 4:9, 12-13). After all, they, too, faced external conflict and hardship (1:25, 27-30; 2:17-18).[10] And Paul rejoiced in the Philippians' material gift, delivered by Epaphroditus (4:10, 18).

Paul's attitude of joy and his exhortation to rejoice flow from a reaffirmation of the essentials. Believers are to rejoice "in the Lord." It is He, not culture or social standards, who binds them together. Rejoicing flows from His work. His death and resurrection are the common denominators for the community of faith. These very things that enable believers to stand acquitted before a holy God enable them to strive together for the sake of the gospel.

Display Attitudes of Forbearance

We all are capable of wearing our attitudes on our sleeves— sometimes intentionally, sometimes unintentionally. And each of us has certain personality traits that enhance one attitude over another. But as we learn to rejoice in the Lord, we should develop attitudes indicating that Jesus Christ is being formed in us. Paul said to that disunited, status-seeking congregation: "Let your gentleness be evident to all"

(4:5). The Greek word *epieikes* ("forbearance," NASB; "gentleness," NIV), is hard to express in a single English word. The idea is one of gentle forbearance, a sweet reasonableness. According to Paul, this forbearance was a characteristic of Jesus Himself (2 Corinthians 10:1).

Those watching from the outside should be able to see that Christians are different. Our corporate attitude impacts the gospel's effectiveness! In the context of Philippians, this forbearance was contrary to the prideful attitudes that had crept into the congregation. Paul drew upon a Greek word that conveyed a quality of mind that does not insist on its own rights.[11] He said a believer should maintain an attitude that does not put a priority on personal rights.

Paul's reference to Christ's return ("The Lord is near," 4:5) gives this exhortation to gentleness added weight. The sentence, "The Lord is near," carries a dual connotation. On the one hand, since Jesus lives in the midst of His Church, the members ought to exercise forbearance. On the other, since Christians live expecting the return of Jesus (1:6, 10-11; 2:16), we are to facilitate an attitude becoming of His kingdom. Lightfoot understood the dynamics of this command in view of Paul's previous exhortations: "To what purpose is this rivalry, this self-assertion? The end is nigh, when you will have to resign all. Bear with others now, that God may bear with you then."[12]

Make Prayer a Central Aspect of Your Church Community's Life

Paul knew that a prayerless congregation at Philippi would not have the frame of mind to promote harmony among its ranks. Hence, his command: "Do not be anxious about anything, but in everything, by prayer and petition, with thanksgiving, present your requests to God" (4:6).

This command comes in two parts: a prohibition and a positive exhortation. The Philippians had plenty to worry about. They faced external pressure from false missionaries ("evil workers") (3:2, NASB) and from society (1:28-29). They were experiencing internal agitation by those seeking status or with competing self-interests. So Paul exhorts, "Do not be anxious about anything." But the absence of worry is not enough. The vacuum must be filled. For the Philippians and for us, prayer is the great vacuum-filler! Prayer will guard, keep, protect our hearts and minds.

In a single sentence (4:6), Paul uses four different words to describe prayer: "prayer" (*proseuche*), "petition" (*deesis*), "thanksgiving" (*eucharistia*), "requests" (*aitema*). Although it is instructive to know the various modes of prayer, Paul most likely uses this list for rhetorical effect. The congregation was experiencing not peace, but division. To return God's peace to the congregation, Paul recommended prayer—ardent, all-encompassing prayer.

"The peace of God, which transcends all understanding" (4:7) is the antithesis to the anxiety that permeated the congregation. It is not so much that this peace is the *result* of praying, but the peace of God dwells among those who *are* praying. And it is this peace that "stands guard" over the hearts and minds of those who pray.[13]

The Community of Faith Must Seek Excellence in \What It Affirms

Today's trend is toward excellence in ministry. It sounds good—at first. There is nothing wrong with doing things well, or at least to the very best of our ability. But we now seem to have made excellence a fetish. We are so consumer-oriented that we tend to allow only "professionals" (or those who have a professional presence) to minister. This attitude stems from a wrong understanding of what biblical excellence means.

Biblical excellence can refer to the sacrifices needed to enter into God's presence or to obtain His forgiveness. Or excellence can refer to virtues that demonstrate godliness or the gospel. The latter is what Paul is getting at in 4:8-9.

Patrick Morley, author of *The Man in the Mirror,* reflects on his own journey from excellence in the material, consumer world to excellence in godliness. In an interview with Phil Callaway, editor of *Servant Magazine,* Morley confesses:

> In the early '80s I became aware that I had become a cultural Christian. My life had been shaped more by the force of commerce than Christ. I was living out a Christian lifestyle, but I was a materialist. I had married a perfect wife, bought a home, leased a luxury car, bought expensive Hickey-Freeman suits, began numerous real estate partnerships, wore a Rolex watch, and generally thought I had gone to heaven. I was reading my Bible for comfort, but *Forbes* for direction. My big thing was goal-setting. I listened to motivational tapes and read every book ever written on success. I met every goal I set, yet my life seemed hollow. I found success didn't satisfy.[14]

What we affirm as worthy or excellent displays either our trust in the "world" or our faith in Christ. The Church will continue to be unhealthy as long as Christians affirm the world's values. Rather, we should affirm excellent virtues and excellent thinking that build the Church.

Affirm Excellent Thinking
In 4:8, Paul exhorts the Philippians to "think about" (*logizesthe*) a series of virtues. Although NIV translates *logizesthe* "think about," it is not one of the *phroneo* verbs

Paul has used throughout the letter in referring to the Philippians' frame of mind—their thinking. Semantically there is little difference, but Paul here is stressing Christians' need to make a conscious effort. They must *reckon* these virtues as excellent for Christian godliness.

A Measuring Line for Godliness

Paul says, "If anything is excellent or praiseworthy—think about such things." His list of excellent, praiseworthy virtues, demeanors and intentions is a measuring line for godliness. It will help produce harmony and mutual respect in the Church.

Some have questioned whether these virtues are distinctly Christian or basically cultural.[15] Certainly the list of worthy virtues is not complete! Whether essentially cultural or Christian, Paul chooses virtues calculated to achieve unity and foster a mutual commitment to the gospel.

- *Whatever is* true. Truth should characterize the Christian community. The world is filled with falsehoods, from false ideas to false images. The Christian community is to adorn itself with truth, both in its speech and in its actions.
- *Whatever is noble.* The Christian community is to think on things that lift the mind. Noble things are worthy of respect. They represent moral worth.
- *Whatever is right.* Literally, *just.* In our relationships with others we are to evidence mutual respect. Our actions should reflect concern for the other's welfare.
- *Whatever is pure.* The word *pure* has a wide range of meaning. Biblical purity is often associated with "good thoughts." The Christian community should evidence high motives and the best of intentions. This will enhance mutual respect. It

will foster unity of purpose.
- *Whatever is lovely.* The word *lovely* is used but once in the New Testament—here in 4:8. Other translations render it *pleasing* (NRSV) or *admirable* (NASB, NEB). The idea is "a friendly disposition."[16] Christians are to exhibit genuine admiration and friendly affection for each other. Their activities are to elicit grace rather than bitterness or hostility.
- *Whatever is admirable.* Again, the word is used only here in the New Testament. It denotes the kind of conduct well spoken of by other people. Christians are to show mutual respect. They are to put aside selfish attitudes that could offend others. They are to be winsome. Their activities should be those that others will respect, appreciate and acknowledge as good.

These Are "Action" Virtues: Put Excellence into Practice

These virtues are associated with action (as the descriptions imply). Paul's whole letter has been an exhortation to the Philippians to "think," to have a certain "frame of mind," a specific attitude. But in case any reader supposed that thinking was only a cognitive pursuit, Paul exhorts all his recipients to follow *his* actions. We are to practice the above virtues.

In keeping with the "model" paradigm Paul has presented throughout the letter, he offers himself as a pattern for the Philippians to follow. "Whatever you have learned or received or heard from me, or seen in me—put it into practice. And the God of peace will be with you" (4:9).

This exhortation brings to mind what Paul wrote earlier in the letter: "For it has been granted to you on behalf of Christ not only to believe on him, but also to suffer for him, since you are going through the same struggle you saw

I had, and now hear that I still have" (1:29-30).

What in Paul are the Philippians to emulate? His *joy.* His *perseverance.* His *love for the brethren.* His *sacrifice for the gospel and the Church.* All of these for sure—and more. The apostle has demonstrated in the letter that he had a single mind when it came to the work of the gospel. Luke implies as much in his writing about Paul in Acts. We are to practice Paul's virtues through our love for the Church and in our working together with others for the sake of the gospel. We are to practice this "frame of mind" by the way we define our Christian life and our Church life. The surrounding culture is not to be our standard. Rather, the cross and Jesus' resurrection from the dead are our standards.

If the "God of peace" is to dwell in the Church today, self-interest must die. Mutual respect must take its place. This peace that God brings is the complete opposite of the prideful and self-seeking attitudes that are destroying the Church and weakening the effectiveness of the gospel.

But, again, it is not simply peace that we need, but the *God* of peace. Someone has called the Church the visible sign of salvation that God has established in this seemingly godless world. No wonder Paul considered the spiritual health of the Philippian church so important!

To Be Genuine, the Community of Faith Needs to Go Against the Cultural Flow

Surely we must undertake the application of the grace of God in the Church. In a given local church, however, there will be various levels of Christian progress. Christians are not born mature! Neither do we enter into the life of Christ through a system of rules and regulations. Granted, there is a starting point, variously known as salvation, justification, the new birth. But once in the family of God, healthy Christian character is formed as the believer participates in the community of faith.[17] This most definitely calls for teamwork (4:2-3; Ephesians 4:1-16).

Every Christian, but especially the leadership (cf. 1:1; 3:15), must explain in word and demonstrate through example the importance of the church—their church. Activities and policies must foster *community.* Some ministries and some attitudes may need to be reevaluated. So be it!

There must be conscious, willing, mindful commitment for the church community to seek health. I am not speaking of the Church universal, but of the local church— your church. Marva Dawn has written *Reaching Out without Dumbing Down: A Theology of Worship for the Turn-of-the-Century Culture.* When it comes to restoring the church's health, the author notes the difficulty, but the necessity to be counterculture. She writes:

> In the first place, most churches fail to admit how much they have to go against the cultural flow to become a genuine community; and second, few are willing to expend the effort it takes to develop the necessary commitment.[18]

Difficult? Yes. Urgent? Absolutely. Paul had that conviction as he wrote to the first-century Christians in Philippi. If he were present today, his resolve would be as steadfast.

Endnotes

[1] First Corinthians 8-9 and Second Corinthians 10-12, where Paul indicates a more faithful, a more biblical model for understanding freedom.

[2] Other similar *paraenesis* (hortatory) sections in Paul's letters: Romans 12:1ff; Galatians 5:1ff; Ephesians 4:1ff; Colossians 3:1ff; 1 Thessalonians 4:1ff.

[3] From the author's hand-written notes; original source

unknown.

[4] Gordon Fee, *Paul's Letter to the Philippians* (Grand Rapids, MI: Eerdmans, 1995), 389-390. Also, Moises Silva, *Philippians* (Chicago, IL: Moody, 1988), 221.

[5] Silva, 222.

[6] Robert Bellah, et. al., *Habits of the Heart: Individualism and Commitment in American Life* (Berkeley,CA: University of California Press, 1985), 6.

[7] C.S. Lewis, *The Screwtape Letters* (Westwood, NJ: Barbour and Company, 1961), 81-82.

[8] For other New Testament references to the book of life, see Revelation 3:5; 20:15; 21:27.

[9] E.M. Bounds, *Power through Prayer,* ed. Penelope J. Stokes (Minneapolis, MN: World Wide Publications, 1989), 13.

[10] Fee, 405-406.

[11] Gerald F. Hawthorne, *Word Biblical Commentary,* Vol. 43, *Philippians* (Waco, TX: Word, 1983), 182.

[12] J.B. Lightfoot, *St. Paul's Epistle to the Philippians* (Grand Rapids, MI: Zondervan, 1965), quoted by Silva, 225.

[13] Hawthorne, 184. Note that Jesus' own teaching on prayer relates to how Christians maintain a proper attitude in the world and amid their relationships with others (Matthew 6:25, 32; Luke 12:22, 30).

[14] An interview with Patrick Morley by Phil Callaway in *Servant* Magazine (Prairie Bible Institute, Winter 1996), 10.

[15] Primarily Christian virtues, Silva, 229; basically Jewish wisdom, Fee, 415; essentially common civic values, Hawthorne, 187-188.

[16] Fee, 418.

[17] Marva J. Dawn, *Reaching Out without Dumbing Down: A Theology of Worship for the Turn-of-the-Century Culture* (Grand Rapids, MI: Eerdmans, 1995), 116.

[18] Ibid., 131.

CHAPTER 12

Life on the Cutting Edge of Service

Philippians 4:10-23

WHAT WOULD IT TAKE, REALLY TAKE, TO make you content? to make you happy? to make you satisfied?

A fancy pickup truck, stocked with all the options, passed me on Interstate 95. My ancient mini-truck was dwarfed by its size and flamboyance. I had a sense of feeling cheated. There I was, put-putting along in my multicolored, used '74 Chevy Luv. And there was this guy, flashing by me in his shiny new behemoth.

As he passed I noticed a bumper sticker neatly pasted to the chrome rear bumper. *He who dies with the most toys wins.* As far as the world with its passionate pursuits was concerned, I was the obvious loser.

But I in my aging pickup knew something that fellow didn't. Perhaps I should say I knew *Someone* he didn't. When life consists of items of purchase and the fulfillment of temporal pleasures, the result is meaninglessness. The writer of Ecclesiastes cautions us to be careful where we look for contentment:

> *So my heart began to despair over all my toilsome labor under the sun. For a man may do his work with wisdom, knowledge and skill, and then he must leave all he owns to someone who has not worked for it. This too is meaningless and a great misfortune. What does a man get for all the toil and anxious striving with which he labors under the sun? All his days his work is pain and grief; even at night his mind does not rest. This too is meaningless.* (Ecclesiastes 2:20-23)

I am amazed at the attitudes of my contemporaries. I am even more aghast because so many among the community of faith have been seduced by similar attitudes. Whether it is instant success, material affluence, or bigger and better churches, we believers can be accused of exchanging the Christ-life for life as the world defines it.

I am not a fan of Christian designer tee shirts. Much of what is plastered on them comes close to sacrilege. But I was pleasantly surprised by one shirt that mocked the boastful arrogance of that trucker's life verse. It read: *He who dies with the most toys still dies.*

A Vital Truth

That slogan catches the essence of a vital truth. Christians, of all people, ought to know that this world and the things of this world are passing away (1 Corinthians 7:31; 1 John 2:15-17; Matthew 7:24-29). Yet we have fashioned our criteria for meaningful spirituality and meaningful church life from the world's models. Affluence and the American ideas of success and freedom are what count. But death, the common denominator, will expose our vanity in striving for the wind—striving for a world-given, culture-driven contentment.

I ask the question again. What will it take to make you content?

Perhaps our problem is rooted in how we *become* content. We have reduced contentment to its lowest common denominator—items we buy and feelings of comfort. Paul's final words to the church at Philippi raise the Christian idea of contentment to its proper sphere. True contentment flows from a commitment to something worthy, something eternal, something beyond us. True contentment flows from a commitment to the gospel.

We have come to the exhortative section of this letter in 4:1-20. The last half of it (4:10ff) is highly informative regarding Christian contentment. Before this the apostle exhorted his readers to imitate his life (3:17; 2:17-18; 3:4-14). He says it again in 4:9: "Whatever you have learned or received or heard from me, or seen in me—put it into practice."[1] There is no doubt that in this closing section, Paul continues to suggest that *he has modeled the authentic Christian life,* the deeper life.

Restless Christians struggling to find contentment give rise to a self-interest mentality within church communities. That, in turn, results in ill health for the Body of Christ. In 4:10-19, however, we discover a strong and dynamic connection between Christians' level of contentment and their commitment to the gospel.

We Must Learn the Power of Commitment to the Gospel

Paul has come full circle. He began his letter by expressing his thankfulness for the Philippian congregation.

> *I thank my God every time I remember you. In all my prayers for all of you, I always pray with joy because of your partnership* [koinonia; participation, NASB] *in the gospel*

from the first day until now. (1:3-5; cf. 1:7)

That quality of thankfulness and joy runs the length of the letter. Always it is linked to the Philippians' partnership with Paul in gospel proclamation. This is very counter to the present-day preoccupation with personal gratification and the promotion of self-interests.

There may be no better example of this than our contemporary approach to church life and church growth. Paul, as we have seen, has been concerned with the advancement of the gospel and its impact on both unsaved and saved (1:12, 25, 27; 2:15, 22; 4:3). Our contemporary, market-driven church growth, and church life focuses on the individual. As a result, our church life and our individual spirituality are one-dimensional. We find ourselves living in isolation, not community.

Some are now noticing the disparity. We expend huge sums of emotional energy as well as human and material resources to attract the baby boomers and busters. In doing so, we have strangled the resources for global missions and concerns of social justice. Our current emphasis is on meeting consumer needs (not necessarily the same thing as "felt need"). We may deny it, but we cannot help but ask the question: *How popular can we be?* The Church is held hostage by current trends and the self-interests of its adherents.

In this final section of Paul's letter, he displays his own frame of mind regarding contentment in the Christian life. We hear him again expressing gratitude for the gifts and supplies sent by the Philippians to meet his personal and ministry needs. But he also uses the occasion to model true contentment for a church consumed by anxiety (1:28-30; 4:6-7) and bent on self-interests (2:1-4, 12).

We need to put these final exhortations into their proper perspective. Paul was *not* ultimately concerned about the Christians' personal contentment. His supreme concern was for the vitality of the local church and the advancement of the gospel. And by extension Paul corrects *our* frame of mind about contentment in order to bring health back to *our* churches. We too must understand that our contentment is related to our commitment to the gospel. True contentment will raise our church life above depressing circumstances and harmful affliction.

Our Level of Commitment Determines Our Level of Contentment

What contributes to our discontent? our restlessness? Three often suggested culprits are material affluence, self-centeredness, and our success orientation. We acknowledge the validity of the observations. Yet we continue to indulge. The contemporary ideas of "fulfillment" and the consumer environment (material affluence) are powerful influences on our dispositions and habits.

We live in an environment of choice. *Choice* has become the most operative word in our society. As Christians we may be appalled by the advocates of abortion choice or lifestyle choice or entertainment choice. But we too enjoy the pluralistic nature of our culture. It offers us freedom, power, fulfillment. Living in such a milieu actually works against our contentment for the things of the gospel.

In his book *A Far Glory,* Peter Berger underscores the tensions created by pluralism—the multitude of options we face. He points out how these choices are ingrained in our cultural experience. Berger looks on pluralism as a social state of affairs. Society multiplies our choices at every level, whether the choices are commercial or ideas. This makes it very difficult to maintain unique, distinct and deeply held convictions about anything.[2]

Our problem is that we are almost forced to view Christianity within the framework of pluralism. And this reveals, at least partially, the reason for most of our discontentment—with God, with church and with the Christian life. We will not see this remedied until we stop viewing Christianity as a choice.

Paul used the matter of giving and receiving to help the Philippian congregation rid itself of anxiety (4:6-7) and cure itself of the perils of self-interests (2:1-4). He writes:

> *I rejoice greatly in the Lord that at last you have renewed your concern for me. Indeed, you have been concerned, but you had no opportunity to show it.* (4:10)

Paul was responding to their kind gift that supplied his needs while he was under house arrest. Likely they sent food, clothing, possibly money, and perhaps reading material. The evident delay in the gift's arrival may have been due to their financial lack. It is also possible that Epaphroditus, the messenger, became ill while *en route* to Rome (cf. 2:25ff).

Most English translations mask an important Greek phrase Paul uses to acknowledge the Philippians' gift. The words *your concern for me* are derived from Paul's frequently used word for "thinking"—*phonein.*[3] Without making 4:10 too wooden-literal, Paul was saying, "I greatly rejoice in the Lord that at last you are thinking rightly by ministering to my needs for the cause of the gospel." In other words, they were right in thinking about Paul in this way.[4]

Although Paul appreciated their gift, his joy came from their frame of mind that led them to share, once again, in the advancement of the gospel. That moved Paul to use this occasion to explain true Christian contentment. He uses his own life as the model.

True Contentment Rises above Circumstances
At first glance it might appear that Paul did not think very

highly of the Philippians' gift. He says in 4:11: "I am not saying this because I am in need, for I have learned to be content whatever the circumstances." The gift from the Philippians was good not just because it met Paul's need, but because it showed a hopeful turn of attitude for the church in Philippi. It indicated that they could rise above their circumstances to demonstrate appropriate Christian thinking.

Paul was saying, in effect, "Yes, I had legitimate needs that your gift supplied, but it is not the gift that causes me to rejoice. I rejoice because you gave. You rose above your anxiety and self-interests to minister for the gospel's sake. For you see, I too have learned to rise above my circumstances. And this has led me to be content no matter the circumstances."

Today Christian life and church life are not built on any real sense of objectivity. This has turned everything on its head. Admittedly, the self-focus that characterizes much of church life and church growth today has been highly successful. But it has come at a high cost. We advise both believers and the unchurched to seek assurance in subjective experience of the gospel rather than objective truth. We teach them to ask, *Does it meet my needs?* Not, *Is it true?* Paul's personal testimony reminds us that we must temper experience with the gospel's objective nature. Without such a truth reference for our lives, contentment will ebb and flow with each succeeding circumstance.

Recall Paul's first words in this paragraph: "I rejoice greatly in the Lord" (4:10). This joy in the Lord helps us to understand how Paul is able to rise above his circumstances. There is something objective that is always outside his situation, something that remains constant. The phrase *rejoice in the Lord* reminds us of Paul's constant recollection of the power and joy in the gospel. It is the gospel that provides the objective means and the power to rise above circumstances. Our ability to be content is directly linked to our level of commitment to the gospel.[5]

True Commitment Is a Learned Experience

Paul continues his remarks about contentment in 4:12-13. He explains that it comes by experience. He had *learned* to be content, both when he had plenty and when he was wanting.

When Paul admits, "I know what it is to be in need," he is alluding to his effort to be like Jesus in His humility. He uses the word *tapeinousthai* for what the various translations render "need," "want," "poverty." It is the same word Paul used to describe Jesus' *humble* choice to leave His privileged position in heaven to become a man.[6] Elsewhere, Paul uses the same word to indicate that his lifestyle is similar to, or an imitation of, his Lord's (1 Corinthians 4:11-13; 2 Corinthians 6:4-5; 11:23-29; 4:8-9).[7]

Do not misread Paul's word *plenty.* We are inclined to imagine it in terms of our affluent material abundance. Paul was likely referring to the Philippians' gift.[8] He was saying, in reality, "I have learned to be content with the gifts that have been graciously supplied by people like yourselves."

Think back. Have you ever been given a gift and thought to yourself, *This is not enough* or *So-and-so got more?* Even when we receive, we can tend to think we deserve more or better. But that is not the way to learn contentment. We learn contentment by rejoicing when we receive anything that supplies our needs.

So Paul was not talking just about material affluence or its lack. He had learned to be content in his position as a servant of the Lord Jesus Christ. He had learned contentment because he had given himself to a lifestyle that centered on the gospel. And this lifestyle put him in circumstances where he was deprived of needs. Moreover, he had learned to be content whether or not those needs were met. The ancient Agur understood this principle. He prayed:

> *Two things I ask of you, O LORD*
>> *do not refuse me before I die:*
>>> *Keep falsehood and lies far from me;*
>>>> *give me neither poverty nor riches,*
>>>> *but give me only my daily bread.*
>> *Otherwise, I may have too much and disown you*
>> *and say, "Who is the LORD?"*
> *Or I may become poor and steal,*
>> *and so dishonor the name of my God.*
>>>>>> (Proverbs 30:7-9)

Contentment comes in learning to live as one committed to a lifestyle worthy of the gospel (Phil 1:27).

True Contentment Is Found in Participating in the Gospel

Elsewhere in his correspondence, Paul indicates his self-sufficiency (2 Corinthians 11:23-29). But this is not an arrogant attitude. As one writer put it, Paul was able to be self-sufficient because he was totally committed to the All-Sufficient One. Paul says here, "I can do everything through him who gives me strength." Thus the secret of contentment is dependence—dependence on God.

This verse has suffered at the hands of our contemporary, privatized faith. We read it through the lens of our North American experience. Because we are often seeking to be fulfilled and free and successful, we can misread the text. Often it comes out this way: "I, myself, can do any and everything through Him who is all powerful and gives me the strength to succeed at whatever I put my hand to." That is more a revelation of our modern attitude than a true understanding of Paul's intention.

When Paul says "I can do everything," he did not mean every single thing possible. He meant he could deal with "all things [*panta*]" (NASB) that came his way while he served the Church and participated in the work of the gospel.[9]

This understanding is further underscored by Paul's use of the word *endunamoun*. Literally it means "I have the power to," or, "I am able to." Paul wrote to the Ephesians, "Be strong in the Lord and in his mighty power" (Ephesians 6:10; cf. 6:11). Paul told Timothy he had been strengthened by Christ "because He considered me faithful, putting me into service" (1 Timothy 1:12, NASB). And in a later letter, he encouraged Timothy to "be strong in the grace that is in Christ Jesus" (2 Timothy 2:1). Paul was well aware that Timothy would encounter suffering and hardship as he ministered the gospel.

Paul spoke to Timothy from experience. He himself had frequent need to call on that source of power. Referring to his civil trial, Paul says, "The Lord stood at my side and gave me strength, so that through me the message might be fully proclaimed and all the Gentiles might hear it" (2 Timothy 4:17). Paul found strength for ministry in the strength of his Lord.

Philippians 4:13 is quoted to promote success in everything from business and sports to education and other self-fulfilling endeavors. Those are misuses of the Scripture. Power—and Spirit-given contentment—are granted to those who harness their lives for the advancement of the gospel, not the advancement of self.

Contentment Enables the Local Church to Rise above Circumstances

Paul's model for contentment quickly moves from personal to corporate. We must keep in mind that the health and welfare of the local church is the issue Paul addresses in this letter. He goes on: "Yet it was good of you to share in my troubles" (4:14).

Paul uses a supercharged word to refer to their sharing in his ministry troubles. It is the word *sugkoinonesantes*. You will recognize the word *koinonia*, "fellowship," in the center of it. This verb is built on the word *koinonia*. Paul draws on his previous references to fellowship, partnership, and participation in the gospel (1:5, 7-11). Throughout the letter he has spoken of their sharing in his ministry (1:7, 29-30; 2:17) and especially here in 4:10-19. Out of their own "poverty" (2 Corinthians 11:8-9) they gave to the furtherance of the gospel by providing for Paul's needs. He tells them,

> *As you Philippians know, in the early days of your acquaintance with the gospel, when I set out from Macedonia, not one church shared with me in the matter of giving and receiving, except you only; for even when I was in Thessalonica, you sent me aid again and again when I was in need.* (4:15-16)

Once again Paul expresses gratitude for the Philippians' gift. But it is not the gift that is the final object of his appreciation. He adds: "Not that I am looking for a gift, but I am looking for what may be credited to your account" (4:17).

Paul was applying an ancient, inspired principle in God's kingdom: Obedience is better than sacrifice (1 Samuel 15:22; 51:16-17; Isaiah 1:11-20; Hosea 6:6).[10] The New English Bible puts it this way: "I do not mean to say that I have set my heart on the gift." Paul was acknowledging the Philippians' decision to rise above their "severe trial" and "extreme poverty" (2 Corinthians 8:2) to participate in the gospel. That is the Church's task! Personal contentment and church health are restored when each congregation commits itself to advance the gospel.

A Commercial-Economic Overtone
There was also a commercial-economic ring to Paul's comment about their gift. The NASB translates the latter

half of 4:17: "but I seek for the profit which increases your account." The profit is literally the fruit (*karpon*) that will result from their continued share in advancing the gospel.[11] And of course there will be eternal reward as well. Throughout the letter, Paul has been concerned for their own advance in the faith (1:25; 2:16; 4:1).[12] Homer Kent catches Paul's intention in his interpretation of this text:

> Paul's readers must not suppose that he is primarily concerned with their gift as such, but rather in the development of the grace of giving among them...Their spiritual growth was the fruit Paul desired, and to this end he directed his ministry.[13]

Paul was ultimately concerned about their spiritual growth, not his well-being. The implication, then, is that the "account" we should be most concerned about is not our earthly bank account (that is, our economic survival), but the divine account in heaven (3:20; Matthew 6:19-24).

Paul received from the Philippians everything he needed (Philippians 4:18). He described this gift as "a fragrant offering, an acceptable sacrifice, pleasing to God." It demonstrated to Paul that the Philippians were taking steps to rise above their circumstances. It was a positive move toward corporate spiritual health. Paul elsewhere describes Christ's gift of grace in very similar terms: "Christ loved us and gave himself up for us as a fragrant offering and sacrifice to God" (Ephesians 5:2). The Philippians' gift was of the highest quality; it confirmed to Paul that they had the mind of Christ.[14]

Because of their gift, Paul can assure the Philippians, "My God will meet all your needs according to his glorious riches in Christ Jesus" (4:19).

Again we must ask, What needs? Should we shrink

this to the lowest common denominator of personal, private needs? Of course God will supply our personal needs, as Jesus promised in His Sermon on the Mount (Matthew 6:25-34). But in the context of the letter Paul is about to conclude, he has in mind their "church needs" for spiritual health.[15] This text, despite those who would privatize it, seeks to raise our lives above petty rivalry, the search for self-fulfillment, the satisfying of our self-interests. It reminds us that true contentment is found in our participation in the gospel.

Conclusion: Keep God's Glory in Mind

Paul could not help ending his exhortation with the ultimate exhortation: "To our God and Father be glory for ever and ever. Amen" (4:20). This benediction separates Christianity from everything else: from other religions, from our culture, from our individual self-interests. It is God's glory that we seek, not out own.

When Paul wrote this letter, likely in the early 60s, the only glory having government approval was Caesar's glory—his throne, his dominion, his power and honor. But it is not an earthly, temporal potentate that we glorify. It is the Creator God—our God and Father. It is His glory that we promote. It is the good news of His Son, our Savior, which we proclaim. It is by the strength of His indwelling Holy Spirit that we stand firm. Caesar's glory died when he died. He could not even take it with him to the grave. By contrast, God's glory is forever and ever. Our allegiance is to the eternal God.

Paul's benediction moves us past the earthly concerns that plague us and our churches. It fixes our eyes on eternal verities.

Do Not Overlook the Greetings

The letter has ended with the benediction. But not quite.

Frequently we overlook the greetings at the end of Paul's letters. We suppose they have little relevancy to us. But Paul often used his greetings to reemphasize the major concerns of the letter. The greetings at the end of Philippians are no exception:

> *Greet all the saints in Christ Jesus. The brothers who are with me send greetings. All the saints send you greetings, especially those who belong to Caesar's household. The grace of the Lord Jesus Christ be with your spirit.* (4:21-23)

A person cannot escape the literary finesse of these closing verses. First, Paul emphasizes the joint partnership of the "saints." It is to these "saints" that "the grace of the Lord Jesus Christ" is to be manifested. Yes, the reference to "your spirits" is intended to mean each one's own spirit. But we cannot forget that Paul has already exhorted the Philippians to "stand firm in one spirit, contending as one man for the faith of the gospel" (1:27). We remember that their "fellowship with the Spirit" is to produce persevering joy (2:1-2).

Even as he concludes, Paul pushes the whole Philippian congregation toward persevering joy through participation in the task of the gospel. Paul's high view of the Church and his desire for its health is pivotal to the advancement of the gospel. He refers to the Christians in "Caesar's household." He is subtly saying that despite the Church's conflict with Caesar, the gospel has penetrated Caesar's imperial palace.

Restore Your Persevering Joy by Habit-forming Obedience

That leaves us with a final question. How do we make this kind of a commitment to the gospel of Jesus Christ and His local church?

In his novel *Cold War in Hell*, Harry Blamires describes English villagers exiting a quaint chapel after Sunday Evensong. Lamiel, an angel, and an unnamed, still-skeptical companion are observing the scene.[16] Their conversation goes like this:

> "That is a good thing to see," said Lamiel.
>
> I thought [Lamiel's comment] rather a sentimental utterance. . . . I decided to take him up on it.
>
> "Can we really decide whether it is a good thing, when we don't know what these people are thinking or feeling?" I asked.
>
> "We can indeed," Lamiel replied.
>
> "But suppose they go to church only because they think it is the proper thing to do?" . . .
>
> "What better reason is there for going to church? Would you have them go on the grounds that it is an improper thing to do?" . . .
>
> "Well," I said, "for all we know, they may have sat through a church service, paying very little attention to what they said or to what was said to them."
>
> "Knowing human beings," said Lamiel, "I should think that almost certain to be the case."
>
> "Then isn't it very hypocritical?"
>
> "Nonsense," said Lamiel. "It is merely human, in a justifiable sense of that much-abused word...They certainly cannot live at a feverish level of intellectual concen-

tration or spiritual activity for more than a few moments at a time. They must necessarily go through a great deal of unanalyzed repetition in the course of public worship. Does that detract from the value of their worship?"

"Their hearts ought to be in it—" I began, but Lamiel interrupted me.

"Their hearts are most certainly in it, or they wouldn't be there. They'd be in a pub instead. Let me ask you a question. Suppose your son comes into your room in the evening before he goes to bed. And suppose he says, 'Good night, Father.' Would you stop him and rebuke him, asking, 'My boy, did you really mean that? Was your heart in it?' Of course not. His heart is in it, for he does it. He does it because he knows it is the proper thing to do. . . . In the same way, men go to church not only because they wish to worship God, but in order that they may wish to worship God."

Lamiel understood the necessity of practicing that which is proper in order to nourish obedience in the heart and life. Paul said, "I have learned to be content whatever the circumstances" (4:11). We learn to be content by being content. We learn obedience by being obedient. We learn to be unselfish by being unselfish.

Committing Ourselves to the Gospel

As a pastor, I saw people come and go—like the wind, like the tide. I was the most skeptical of those who bulldoze into my office declaring, "God has led me here!" They sound spiritual. But I usually discover an attitude that seeks self-fulfillment above the good of the congregation. As soon as any restrictions or limitations are mentioned— or they hear of better opportunities elsewhere—they're gone. Rare are the words: "I believe God would have me make a commitment to this church—despite how I feel or the condition of the church."

Commitment to anything is hard. Commitment to Church life is harder yet, for everything—our human nature and our culture—works against such staying-power commitment. But we all need to start somewhere.

Why not start with some habit-forming, character-developing commitments? First, commit yourself to attend regularly one church—only one. Before long, you will discover other commitments that you need to make: serving, praying and eventually—as God opens the opportunity— leading.

Commit yourself to church life—to *a* church's life. It is necessary if your own spirituality is to be revived. It is necessary for the health of the Church—your church. You must make decisions that produce life-long character traits which run counter to cultural expectations.

David Wells concludes his book *God in the Wasteland* with an exhortation befitting contemporary Christian men and women. He writes:

> If it is for God, for His truth, for His people, for the alienated and trampled in life, then [the Church] must give up what the post-modern world holds most dear. It must give up the freedom to do anything it happens to desire. It must give up self-cultivation for self-surrender, entertainment for worship, intuition for truth, slick marketing for authentic witness, success for faithfulness, power for humility, a God bought on cheap

terms for the God who calls us to a costly obedience. It must, in short, be willing to do God's business on God's terms. As it happens, that idea is actually quite old, as old as the New Testament itself, but in today's world it is novel all over again.[17]

Persevering joy can be restored to our lives and the life of our churches. But it will not come through the instant cash machine or the fast-food restaurants or our pluralistic, privatized North American frame of mind.

It will come when we submit to the Lordship of Jesus Christ and commit ourselves to the welfare of His Church—our church.

Endnotes

[1] Gordon Fee, *Paul's Letter to the Philippians* (Grand Rapids, MI: Eerdmans, 1995), 427.

[2] For two very good volumes on the effects of pluralism and pluralization, especially as they relate to the Church, see Peter Berger, *A Far Glory* (New York: The Free Press, 1992) and Os Guinness, *The Gravedigger File* (Downers Grove, IL: InterVarsity, 1983).

[3] Gerald F. Hawthorne, *Word Biblical Commentary*, Vol. 43, *Philippians* (Waco, TX: Word, 1983), 196.

[4] Fee, 429.

[5] See Marva J. Dawn, *Reaching Out without Dumbing Down: A Theology of Worship for the Turn-of-the-Century Culture* (Grand Rapids, MI: Eerdmans, 1995), 110.

[6] Tapeinoun, "to humble" (2:8). See Fee, 432.

[7] Fee, 433.

[8] Ibid.

[9] "All things" (NASB) or "everything" (NIV) refers to "all those situations mentioned above" (Hawthorne, 201).

[10] Moises Silva, *Philippians* (Chicago: Moody, 1988), 239.

[11] Fee, 437.

[12] Ibid., 447.

[13] Homer A. Kent, *Philippians, The Expositor's Bible Commentary*, Vol. 11, ed. Frank E. Gaebelein (Grand Rapids, MI: Zondervan, 1981), 156.

[14] Hawthorne, 207.

[15] Ibid.

[16] Harry Blamires, *Cold War in Hell* (Nashville, TN: Thomas Nelson, 1955), 25-27. The story line involves the book's skeptical "I," a writer who wonders "how to get to heaven," and an angel companion, Lamiel, who seeks to convey to him "heaven's point of view."

[17] David Wells, *God in the Wasteland: The Reality of Truth in a World of Fading Dreams* (Grand Rapids, MI: Eerdmans, 1994), 223.

Bibliography

Alexander, Donald. *Christian Spirituality: Five Views of Sanctification.* Downers Grove, IL: InterVarsity, 1988.

Anderson, Chip M. "An Investigation of *en pneumati* (in Spirit) in Ephesians 5:18 Within a Conceptual and Linguistic Framework." Paper presented at the 45th annual meeting of the Evangelical Theological Society, 1993.

_____ "Romans 1:1-5 and the Purpose of Romans: The Solution to the Two-Congregation Problem in Rome." *Trinity Journal* (14NS, No 1): 25-40.

Bell, James. *Bridge over Troubled Waters: Ministry to Baby Boomers, a Generation Adrift.* Wheaton, IL: Victor Books, 1993.

Bellah, Robert N., et. al. *Habits of the Heart: Individualism and Commitment in American Life.* New York: Harper and Row, 1985.

Berger, Peter. *A Far Glory.* New York: The Free Press, 1992.

Black, David Alan and David S. Dockery, eds., *New Testament Criticism and Interpretation.* Grand

Rapids, MI: Zondervan, 1991.

Blamires, Harry. *Cold War in Hell*. Nashville, TN: Thomas Nelson, 1955.

Bonhoeffer, Dietrich. *The Cost of Discipleship*. New York: Macmillan Publishing Co., 1976.

Bounds, E. M. *Power through Prayer,* Penelope J. Stoles, ed. Minneapolis, MN: World Wide Publications, 1989.

Bubna, Paul F. *Second Corinthians: Ministry: God at Work in Me for the Good of Others*. Camp Hill, PA: Christian Publications, 1993.

Colson, Charles. *The Body: Being Light in Darkness*. Dallas, TX: Word, 1992.

Crichton, Michael, *Jurassic Park*. New York: Ballantine Books, 1993.

Dawn, Marva J. *Reaching Out without Dumbing Down: A Theology of Worship for the Turn-of-the-Century Culture*. Grand Rapids, MI: Eerdmans, 1995.

"Democracy's Next Generation." Washington: People for the American Way, 1989.

DeSilva, David A. "No Confidence in the Flesh: The Meaning and Function of Philippians 3:2-21," *Trinity Journal* 15NS (1994): 27-54.

Edwards, Jonathan. *The Works of Jonathan Edwards,* Vol. I, Henry Rogers, ed., revised by Edward Hickman. London: Ball, Arnold and Co., 1840.

Fee, Gordon. *Paul's Letter to the Philippians*. Grand Rapids, MI: Eerdmans, 1995.

Gaffin, Richard. *Resurrection and Redemption: A Study in Paul's Soteriology*. Phillipsburg, NJ: Presbyterian and Reformed Publishing Co., 1987.

Glendon, Mary Ann. *Rights Talk: The Impoverishment of Political Discourse*. New York, NY: Free, 1991.

Guinness, Os. *Fit Bodies, Fat Minds: Why Evangelicals Don't Think and What to Do about It*. Grand Rapids, MI: Baker, 1994.

_____ *The American Hour: A Time of Reckoning and the Once and Future Role of Faith.* New York: The Free Press, 1993.

_____ *The Dust of Death: A Critique of the Counter Culture.* Downers Grove, IL: InterVarsity, 1973.

_____ *The Gravedigger File.* Downers Grove, IL: InterVarsity Press, 1983.

Guinness, Os and John Seel, eds. *No God but God: Breaking with the Idols of Our Age.* Chicago, IL: Moody, 1993.

Hawthorne, Gerald F. *Philippians. Word Biblical Commentary,* Vol. 43. Waco, TX: Word, 1983.

Horton, Michael. *Beyond Cultural Wars: Is America a Mission Field or a Battlefield?* Chicago: Moody, 1994.

Hunter, James *Evangelicalism: The Coming Generation.* Chicago: University of Chicago, 1987.

Johnson, Paul. *Intellectuals.* New York: Harper & Row, 1990.

_____ *Modern Times: The World from the Twenties to the Eighties.* New York: Harper & Row, 1983.

Kaiser, Walter. *Toward an Exegetical Theology.* Grand Rapids, MI: Baker, 1981.

Kent, Homer A. *Philippians, The Expositor's Bible Commentary,* Vol. 11, Frank E. Gaebelein, ed. Grand Rapids, MI: Zondervan, 1981.

Kim, Seyoon. *The Origin of Paul's Gospel.* Grand Rapids, MI: Eerdmans, 1983.

Kreeft, Peter. *Between Heaven and Hell.* Downers Grove, IL: InterVarsity, 1982.

Leithart, Peter J. "The Politics of Emma's Hand," *First Things,* 51 (March 1995).

Lewis, C.S. *The Screwtape Letters.* Westwood, NJ: Barbour, 1961.

Lightfoot, J. B. *St. Paul's Epistle to the Philippians.* Grand

Rapids, MI: Zondervan, 1965.

Martin, Ralph P. *New Century Bible Commentary, Philippians*. Grand Rapids, MI: Eerdmans, 1980.

_____ *Philippians*. Greenwood, SC: The Attic Press, Inc., 1976.

Miller, Calvin. *The Singer*. Downers Grove, IL: InterVarsity, 1978.

Muggeridge, Malcolm. *Vintage Muggeridge: Religion and Society*, Geoffrey Barlow, ed. Grand Rapids, MI: Eerdmans, 1985.

Mulholland, M. R. "Sociological Criticism," in David Alan Black and David S. Dockery, eds., *New Testament Criticism and Interpretation*. Grand Rapids, MI: Zondervan, 1991.

O'Brien, Peter. *The Epistle to the Philippians*. Grand Rapids, MI: Eerdmans, 1991.

Packer, J. I. *A Quest for Godliness: The Puritan Vision of the Christian Life*. Wheaton, IL: Crossway, 1990.

Schlossberg, Herbert. *Idols for Destruction: Christian Faith and Its Confrontation with American Society*. Nashville, TN: Thomas Nelson, 1983.

Seel, John. *The Evangelical Forfeit: Can We Recover?* Grand Rapids, MI: Baker, 1993.

Servant Magazine. Prairie Bible Institute, Winter 1996.

Silva, Moises. *Philippians*. Chicago: Moody, 1988.

Simpson, A. B. *The Best of A. B. Simpson*. Bailey, Keith M., ed. Camp Hill, PA: Christian Publications, 1987.

Smith, W. M. "Heaven." *Zondervan Pictorial Encyclopedia of the Bible,* Vol. 3. Merrill C. Tenney, ed. Grand Rapids, MI: Zondervan, 1975.

Snyder, Howard. *The Community of the King*. Downers Grove, IL: InterVarsity, 1977.

Tellbe, Mikael. "The Sociological Factors Behind Philippians 3:1-11 and the Conflict at Philippi," *The Journal for the Study of the New Testament* 55 (1994): 97-121.

Theological Dictionary of the New Testament, G. Kittel and G. Friedrich, eds. Grand Rapids, MI: Eerdmans, 1964-76.

Tozer, A. W. "Uses of Suffering," *The Root of the Righteous.* Harrisburg, PA: Christian Publications, 1955.

_____ "About Hindrances," *The Root of the Righteous.* Harrisburg, PA: Christian Publications, 1955.

Vitz, Paul. "Leaving Psychology Behind," in *No God but God: Breaking with the Idols of Our Age,* Os Guinness and John Seel, eds. (Chicago, IL: Moody, 1993), 108.

Wallis, Jim. *Agenda for Biblical People.* New York: Harper and Row, 1976.

Watson, David. *Called and Committed: World-Changing Discipleship.* Wheaton, IL: Harold Shaw, 1982.

Webster, Douglas D. *Selling Jesus: What's Wrong with Marketing the Church.* Downers Grove, IL: InterVarsity, 1992.

Wells, David. *No Place for Truth.* Grand Rapids: Eerdmans, MI,1993.

_____ *God in the Wasteland: The Reality of Truth in a World of Fading Dreams.* Grand Rapids, MI: Eerdmans, 1994.

Wuthnow, Robert. *Christianity in the 21st Century: Reflections on the Challenges Ahead.* New York: Oxford University Press, 1993.

Yankelovich, Daniel, *New Rules: Searching for Self-fulfillment in a World Turned Upside Down.* New York: Bantam, 1982.

Zacharias, Ravi. *Can Man Live Without God?* Dallas, TX: Word, 1994.

About the Author

❧

Chip M. Anderson has degrees from Crown College and Gordon-Conwell Theological Seminary and was ordained by the Christian and Missionary Alliance. He was a professor at Prairie Bible College (Three Hills, Alberta), and as well, an adjunct-instructor at Nyack College. He has written for *Servant Magazine, MetroVoice,* and *The Christian Librarian*; his articles appear in *His Dominion, The Evangelical Journal,* and *Trinity Journal.* Currently he is the Director of Planning at NEON, Inc., a Community Action Agency in Norwalk, CT. He also served as the Chairperson for Southwestern Connecticut's Welfare-to-Work Task Force. Chip lives in Bridgeport, CT with his wife Lisa and four children, Sarah, Amanda, Michael and Robert. Along with preaching the Word, Chip also consults for community-based and faith-based non-profits, as well as, churches on program development, strategic planning, and mission statement development. He is available for speaking and consulting and can be contacted at wntinc@optonline.net.

Printed in the United States
22364LVS00002B/139-207